The Pop Up Anthology 2014

Edited by Janice Windle

Edited by Janice Windle

First Edition

ISBN: 978-1-907435-24-9

Published by Dempsey & Windle

August 2014

Cover design by Janice Windle and Dónall Dempsey

dempseyandwindle.co.uk

DEDICATION

This book is dedicated to all the people who support
POP-UP POETRY.
That includes the Surrey writers who come to read on our open mic,
the writers from other places who visit at their own expense,
the audiences who encourage our readers and performers
with their attention and applause
(and sometimes by buying their books and CD's),
Sara and the Bar des Arts in Guildford who provide our platform,
the bar staff who sometimes stay up late for us

and it's also dedicated
to Dónall who fed me 'love and barley'
as I edited it

and to you
for buying it.

Foreword

"If a thousand monkeys with a thousand typewriters typed for an infinite length of time, then eventually they would write the complete works of William Shakespeare ..."

Nobody seems quite sure who first made this remark. In any case, we haven't had to go to the animal kingdom or use a thousand laptops to collect the text of this anthology. It seems to us that most people have a poem or two in them, and Pop Up Poets is the group that aims to find and enjoy as many people's poems as we can encourage on to the stage and the page. These poems are far from being the random products of mathematical probability. Personal, honest, crafted with care, or poured joyfully on to the page without inhibition, but never random.

This, the second Pop Up Anthology, celebrates the third year of the series of spoken word and poetry events that we've been running monthly in Guildford. The energy of the group has gone from strength to strength over time; every month new poets and audience have come along to take part in the open mic and listen to the featured poets who give their time and talent so generously, some travelling from far - flung places, including the tropics of Kent, Lincolnshire, Leeds and other counties even further North of Watford, to read and perform for the Surrey audience.

The venue that echoes each month to all these voices is the Bar des Arts, opposite Guildford's Yvonne Arnaud Theatre. We very much appreciate Sara Burks' continued support of the group: the welcoming and yet stylish atmosphere of the Bar des Arts continues to delight visitors and regular performers alike.

Pop Up Poetry was recognized this year as a valued resource for Guildford's Spoken Word community when we were asked to collaborate with the South England Apples and Snakes to curate a section of 'Wordplay', as part of Guildford's Fringe Festival, in the excellent setting of the Bellerby Studio in G-Live.

Three of our recently featured performers read that night: Anna Kahn, Eddie Chauncy and Louise Etheridge, as well as Dónall Dempsey.

We also ran a very successful poetry slam, at the Keystone Pub in Guildford, at the request of Richard Jaehme, as part of the Guildford Fringe Festival.

In the spirit of poetic democracy, which we value as the ethos of our events, every poet who has read at a Pop Up Poetry night has been offered at least one page in this book for their poems. You'll find rants and sonnets, haiku and prose poems, free verse, found poems, rhyming slam poems and love-songs, all co-existing amicably in these pages, just as they do on our platform.

Now read on...

Janice Windle and Dónall Dempsey
Summer 2014

The Poems

The Poems (continued)

The Poems (continued)

The Poems (continued)

STEVE POTTINGER

No-One Likes An Angry Poet

Next Tuesday
what with the weather being lousy
and the nights drawing in
and the rent being due
and the electricity bill hitting the floor
and going through the roof at the same time
and feeling in need of a mid-morning pick me up
to shore up my morale,
I'm going to put on my rain gear
head into town
walk into Starbucks
and smile at the barista.
She'll smile back
because it's good to smile
and I'll order a grande mocha
with an extra shot
a whirl of whipped cream
chocolate sprinkles on top
and to get that sugar hit up and running pronto
I'll have a slab of Chocolate Crunch™
and no, I won't be taking it away.
When she sets it on the counter
I'll give her everything I have
in my pockets.
Sixteen pence in shrapnel,
three washers, one old bus ticket,
and the business card some psychic medium
keeps posting through my door
promising an end to all my worldly ills.
How a man of such prodigious talents
wasn't stopped dead in his tracks
the instant he smashed into the *I don't think so, sunshine*
wall of scepticism just inside the front gate, I'll never know,
but that's another story for another day.
Back in Starbucks
the barista looks puzzled.

She counts up the coins,
hands me back the washers and the bus ticket,
slips the business card into the pocket of her jeans,
smiles,
and tells me I still owe her £5.74.
    I smile back
because no-one likes an angry poet
and I take a deep breath
and I tell her
that as Starbucks has paid no corporation tax
on UK profits for the past three years
I reckon they owe me a couple of hospitals
an old people's home
and an upgrade of our creaking transport system.
    Minus £5.74.
    The barista goes to get the manager.
I take a big slurp of mocha
and a huge bite of Chocolate Crunch™
to keep ahead of the game,
and when he arrives and asks what's going on,
and knowing no-one likes an angry poet,
I give him a big chocolatey grin
and explain about the tax.
Then, before he can whip it away,
I have another gulp of mocha
grab the rest of the Chocolate Crunch™
and stuff it in my gob.
    He threatens to call the police.
There's a long pause.
Partly because my mouth's so full of chocolate
I can barely speak,
but mainly because my response
when it comes
is going to be so densely packed
with fury and expletives
we can't let it loose till well after the watershed
accompanied by some kind of warning
because all this smiling is hard work
and yes, no-one likes an angry poet
but I'm a poet who loves words loves people
and believes some things are worth getting angry about
and if you don't see the difference

between those two
then I probably lost you
soon after I put my rain gear on
back at the start.
    And this is *my* poem.
And in my poem
the customers who've been in here with me
chatting, reading, sheltering from the rain,
they stand as one.
The baristas, tired of working
on their feet all day
throw their aprons to the floor
seize the takings
and march out of the door
and we make our way
from branch to branch
all through town
filling the streets
emptying the tills
into a large sack
which we deliver to the nurses up at A&E.
    We hand out lattes to bus drivers,
fire espressos and carrot cake
into the mouths of homeless people,
give paninis to the unemployed.
Coffee mugs in hand,
chocolate smeared across our faces,
fired up by our belief we're all in this together
and that an injury to one is an injury to all
we storm Vodafone HQ and Amazon UK
for a quiet chat
about the money they owe us,
and as the winter sun
breaks through the clouds
and the windows of the City
are a seamless wall of gold,
I look around,
one poet in a sea of millions
and by god, we're smiling.

KAREN IZOD

Revelation

I hear it before I see it.
There, and there,
that flash of green against hot sandstone,
its camouflage, for the moment, failing to conceal

that this is an ancient route,
a pilgrim's way.
Paths tread deep into the landscape,
slice through a shimmer of time.

The impressions of dusty feet
on a dusty land, are as thoughts
sloughed off, just as cyclists lay waste
their plastic bottles, waiting
for someone to come by and pick them up.

How else might I find myself searching
for the words of an old school hymn,
thinking about the economy of the fields,
the care to cultivate, the measure of it all?

And why does a kind of faith come to mind,
an inclining, a husbandry,
the yoking of a life?
Flayed vines tell of sinew, tendon. Ecce homo
shoulders stretched, staked to the wire.

And round the olive trees necklaces fall,
these ungathered prunings,
not yet set ablaze.

Annual Appraisal

My Ambition is a red dog.
A terrier, always underfoot –
snapping at my heels, circling ankles with her lead.
Off the leash, she could be trotting ahead,
little stubby legs, nose high, ears pricked.
It's the reason I wear those platform heels,
Or appear to hover, about 3 inches off the ground.

My Stretch-Assignment is to grow a twin,
so that when I'm not here, she can take over. 24/7.
Actually, I grow a tail.
It's my Return-on-Investment.
It wags me, rag and tags me.
Not to mention my Eagle Eye for the lies of the land,
helpful for locating a strategic lamp-post, or two.

Never-Never

He lets his hands do the talking now.
Lost boys flitting through an emptying sky.

Silent wrists reach to turn a phrase
through writing-paper skin. Words grasp
at a knuckle, catch on a half-moon.

Palms travel between lap and cheek,
there and back. A no-map journey -
his mouth widens to a stifled 'why?'

Lesson From The Camargue

At the edge of L'Étang de Vacarrés
I contemplate the difference between
a French and an English hard G.

I have to think that it is
the level of salt in the water
that makes you spit out l'étang.

Whereas the viscosity
of a lagoon slops
about inside the mouth.

STEPHEN BOYCE

Knokke Le Zoute

You could hire a kind of go-kart, a squat
four-wheeled pedal bike, and swerve at speed
along the promenade unnerving grannies
or some yapping pooch. Or you could pitch
and roll across the dunes and – furtively -
among the marram grass, observe
the glistening sungirls oil their burnished skin –
disturbing for a twelve-year-old. And when
they headed for the bar or flirted
at the water's edge, you could pour the hot
and honeyed lotion through sandy fingers,
fill up their high-heeled shoes, breathe the dangerous
smell of perfumed leather, swerving
into the clammy mysteries of sex.

Counting The Pips

"O Captain! my Captain! rise up and hear the bells..."
Walt Whitman

I have your three pips on the epaulettes
from your tropical battle dress, packed
in the small back drawer of the military chest
among the assortment of cap badges,
brass buttons and flashes that you kept.

Most mornings I squeeze a lemon into a cup,
add honey and hot water and count the pips
– which I carefully remove with a teaspoon –
as I listen to the weather, time signal, news.

And every day I think of you in singlet
and knee-length khaki shorts, sweating it out
beyond the Brahmaputra, tipping toads
out of your boots, swilling chai in the heat,
hoping not to come face to face with a 'Jap',
and writing letters longing to be home
to care for her, and the little chap –
the first of another three pips, as it turned out.

Vital Signs

Below the tideline on Killiney beach
you shivered as you told me how
the sisters made you bathe in all weathers.

Your words came and went on the breeze
and there among tar and feathers,
cork and wrack, a bloodstone glistened
like a pulsing heart. In my pocket
its sheen of *sang-de-boeuf* soon faded.

We crossed the country in silence.

Rounding the unfinished jigsaw of Galway
and Mayo, I burnished the pebble
in hope it would help you turn back the years.
By Sligo I knew the rose-in-black-rock
blooms only in brine, the salt glaze of tears.

Escapement

I came into the kitchen and the clock was ticking:
you had wound it again into the present tense,

into the fixity of each tooth-clicking second,
sweep of each minute, hour coiled upon hour,

so that we'd act in the moment and that instant
would be shuttered by a circle of numerals,

the matte face no place for pause or reflection;
and what we did now would be done for all time,

no regret, no hesitation, no winding it back,
no parallax error, and everything aligned

in the beat of a heart – like the sudden opening
of a bud beside the straits of Penang,

coinciding precisely with the arrival,
at last, of the slow train to Berrylands.

RICHARD ALLEYNE

Poetry In Brain

I always got poetry in my head.
It usually happens just before I go to bed
and as I go sleep
it checks on me with a little peep.
It's not like a peeping tom,
all it wants to do is keep me informed.
Slowly I doze off and poetry appears again,
this time in a dream,
it just wouldn't go away.
I guess poetry is here to stay.
Poetry, poetry leave me alone!
"No, I can't, I feel at home in your brain,
I'm not trying to drive you insane,
just chilling on your brain."

The Fight

Women fought over the years
with all their might
for equal rights.
Today they came a long way,
but you must be reminded that
you still don't get equal pay
so your fight - is it on hold,
or you're not too bold?
you must let the truth unfold.
There's so much that still has to be told!
I say, get a grip!
Don't let this opportunity slip!
Fight on for your rights!
You graduate with the same degree as he,
doing the same job everyday so I say
you should get equal pay!

INGRID ANDREW

Ingria Andrew<>HeartsSong

Erwin

Leaning

The bus is stranded here, on the road
between three churches,
'God's corner' I have heard it said
I hear the engines low, deep rumble,
the traffic lights are stuck on red.

I see the silent stuccoed church,
the sky above a milky almond green.
No one complains or even murmurs;
into this moment we all lean.

Meantime, a chestnut tree that's in full flower,
sings out the precious transience of the hour.

We all relax into this moment;
no one berates the driver or complains,
we know so much is quite beyond our power
to effect;
oh Bless us all;
and Bless the gently falling, day long
rain.

Spring, From The Bus

Under a spreading, gnarled old plane tree,
from the bus I glimpse this tender sight;
as if in a magic fairy circle,
blue bells, white bells and lilac bells
that shimmer in the damp Spring air,
And fill my mind with lambent light.

GRAHAM BUCHAN

Conjure

Plum with no memory
lies on grass with no aspiration
under sun with no purpose

Those Who Survive

Those who survive
and go on to research documentary films
and go on to make documentary films
and go on to comment on documentary films
and go on to analyse documentary films
and who barely acknowledge (with a gasp of gratitude)
their brush with the bristling skin of oblivion.

Let Us Plant Flowers

Let us plant flowers
    around upright buildings
"I love you very much,
    look after the children."
Let the world trade
   commodities, and currencies
        and aspiration and happiness
"I love you very much,
   look after the children."

My Baby's Got Claws

oh yeah
my baby's got hooves
oh yeah
my baby's got horns
oh yeah
I'm taking my baby BACK TO THE SHOP!
SHE'S NOT WHAT I WANT!

Books

I never quite got lost in
the novels of Jane Austin:
chaste tales of ladies
down on their luck.

No, I was swept by torrents
of D H Lawrence.
At least his girls knew
exactly how to fry an egg

Doubt

I love you so much
it's untrue

The Leader's Wife

The Leader's Wife tried a bit of singing

the Leader's Wife tried a bit of television

the Leader's Wife tried a bit of art

we took the Leader's Wife and tied her to a post

we took the Leader and tied him to a post

opposite

we shot them

slowly

ANON

Justify Your Love

I am quite old now
Compared to lots of you.
Lately I have been really wishing my older relatives were dead.
People like my mother-in-law and even my mother and her old man ....gramps.
It's not that i don't love them... I do… I really love them
I would certainly miss them if they were to go…go to the other side, to pass away, to be no more, to go to their maker and shaker, to die.
The chutney, tea and toiletry sets
At Christmas
And I am sure they are getting the most out of their lives...making chutney, tea and going to pound shops
But they are really more useful to me dead.
It's a difficult position to justify but my credit rating is terrible.

PAUL ECCENTRIC (The Antipoet)

Best Before

Everything I know
I learnt from children's television,
in the sixties and the seventies
before the bad decision
to politicise the children;
make them grow up far too soon,
cast white and black
as good and bad
and tool up their cartoons.
I took compromise
from The Thunderbirds;
and dealt with
Sibling strife,
The Doctor showed me how
to quash the bullies
in my life.
The Wombles taught recycling
and to this day
I can't drop litter,
and Paddington inspired me
to welcome the non fitter.
Captain Scarlet showed that
through adversity we thrive.
It was Catweazle
who showed me how to
adapt and to survive.
But the only thing I've learnt
from children's telly of today
is that killing is alright
if people don't see things your way!

Hanging With Poets

We've spent time in the comp'ny of thespians,
who dropped names with their ev'ry camp breath;
we've been anecdoted to distraction,
we were airkissed and daaahlinked to death.
We've been out with clowns and with jesters;
all manics and miserable blokes,
and they bitched and they sniped at each other
each the butt of the other man's jokes.
We indulged a band of rock minstrels,
we invited their egos to tea,
we pandered and pampered,
They primped, preened and tantrummed,
while admiring themselves on MTV.

So we're quaffing with wordsmiths and ranters;
we're imbibing with poets and bards,
we're rapt in the presence of writers
of the lyrical rebel vanguard.
~we've known doctors and lawyers
and self made employers,
(they've all) shown us the world as they know it;
gen'rals and bureaucrats spouting figures and facts,
(but) we'd much rather be hanging with poets.

We've heard statisticians
and bent politicians
say 'this is the world as we know it',
we've been cleaned out by bankers
and footballing wankers
so we'd rather be hanging with poets.
Yes, we're broke, but we're hanging with poets,
we're broke, 'cause we're hanging with poets.
We're pissed 'cause we're hanging with poets.

BRYAN BAKER

Then And Later

His mother's voice
shooed the ghosts away.
She opened the wardrobe doors, rattled
the coat hangers, showed nothing scary hid there,
even looked under the bed.
Then he slept.

*

The stairs creaked,
he listened,
his hand moved
to the dresser drawer
slipped in, gripped
and withdrew the pistol
then rested it across his chest,
his thumb gently rolled the barrel
its click click brought a memory of comfort,
there there, I'm here now.

When Diane Came To Acton

From Titian's Diana and Actaeon (National Gallery, London).

Yes we did meet, she arrived early.
When I got in the old mutt was asleep as usual.
She's been letting out the most appalling farts lately,
it took some effort to convince Janet it wasn't me.
I heard a female singing,.
There was a splash of water,
the splash it makes around a body, naked in the bath.
The lock doesn't work on that door.
I thought how easy it would be to blunder in.
I'd seen a photo of Diane, she looked very hot.
I stepped over the dog and went lightly up the stairs.
On the landing I waited for her to be quiet,
so my mistake would seem plausible,
when she did, I turned the door handle, heard a gasp
and there she was, naked in the tub,
I was fairly hypnotised by the way her tits floated.
She sprang out all wet, stood in front of me,
nearly six foot of her, shouted something, and drew back her fist,
she looked gorgeous, everything how you'd want.
The punch caught me just above the eye.
She slammed the door. I took a few steps back;
The door flew open; she slung a bottle of aftershave,
it bounced off my head, I missed my footing
and tumbled down the stairs, just missing the dog
who suddenly woke and bit me in the arse; twice,
the same time she let out this loud fart and shat on the carpet,
I didn't realise the second bit until I tried to stand,
skidded, and fell on the dog, who bit me again; in the shin,
then ran off. For a moment I lay there,
smothered by the odour of dog shit, and old spice for men,
I looked up and saw Diane at the top of the stairs,
still without her clothes on, she looked past me,
a racket came from the kitchen as the dog tried to get out
through the cat flap, I craned my neck to see
what she was looking at, and saw Janet in the doorway.

Performance

She sang on a stage at a pub in New Cross,
lit up in front of the crowd. They drank and talked;
from the bar a group shouted the lyrics to her song.

She did her forty minutes and hung up the mic, some applauded
when she stepped down to the bar for one complimentary gin,
with ice, and talked to the barman, no one else. Sometimes,
if the crowd liked her songs, and a man sidled up to her
with the right line of conversation, or humour,
she would take him home. Tonight the crowd were mean

She stepped back on stage for her second half,
took hold of the mic, and sang for the ones who listened;
and after, only to the light, which illuminated her.

On Site

We took a breather under the scaffolding.
Mike's six foot two, fifteen and a half stone, solid,
Recently out after a long stretch, no one asked what for.
Paroled when he agreed to be counselled in temper management.
He says "Hey Bry, how about we head butt the scaffold poles,
Bosh" ... he jerked his head at the scaffolding
Just holding short, "like that" he says, then he did it again "bosh
How about it? just for a laugh,"
I said "sure, go ahead, trouble is,
I'm not very good at that sort of thing,
Most likely I'd only manage a tap."
Something like a shadow crossed his face.
Then it was gone, he lightened, then says "that's alright Bry,
when it comes to your turn
I'll help ya."

SALLY J BLACKMORE

Soldier

I don't know the man who stands
Camouflaged, in green battledress,
Feet apart, straight back, still hands,
Unwitting, not dressed to impress.

Camouflaged in green battledress,
Hard-cropped head turned away,
Unwitting, not dressed to impress,
Despite glossed boots, badged beret.

Hard-cropped head turned away
Exposing bare, vulnerable neck,
Despite glossed boots, badged beret,
Braced shoulders – a flawed effect.

Exposing bare, vulnerable neck,
Pulse rippling beneath soft skin,
Braced shoulders, a flawed effect,
Veiled gaze, attention within.

Pulse rippling beneath soft skin,
My son's rifled brow, drilled with lines,
Veiled gaze, attention within -
Then blue eyes lift, smile into mine.

My son's rifled brow, drilled with lines,
Feet apart, straight back, still hands,
Then blue eyes lift, smile into mine
And I see the boy within the man.

GRAHAM BROWN

Marie-Claire

Marie-Claire you change your hair
more often than your underwear.
One week a lurid green Mohican,
the next an orange Belisha beacon.
Shocking pink, scarlet, zinc, raven black, auburn, mink.

Marie-Claire with face so fair,
a canvas splattered with metalware
not to mention all the studs elsewhere
where no-one looks, they wouldn't dare.
God knows what happens when you fly by air!

Marie-Claire I can but stare
at your tattoos, your shoulder bare
reveals a picture that's unique -
Aubrey Beardsley meets Mervyn Peake
and once by chance I did espy
a skull and crossbones on your thigh.

Marie-Claire, there are those that swear
they have seen the Fighting Temeraire
emblazoned on your derriere
as though you are a sideshow freak
but will you Turner the other cheek –
I have no wish to see your bum!
Marie-Claire, please be aware
you're seventy-five and you are my mum!

Chambermaid

I smile as we pass in the corridor
but only until your back is visible.
Unlocking the door I enter your room,
tolerating your cheap aftershave,
the toenail clippings and the unexplained
stain on the carpet. I replace the coffee sachets
you have stolen and scrub the tea ring
on your bedside table.

You do not deserve clean sheets but still
I neatly fold them over the creaking mattress.
Finally the bathroom. The towels soaked through
from your careless showering are replenished
and the evidence in the cistern has been removed.
I know nothing about the credit card you dropped
beside the bed. Tomorrow I start a new life.

Confidence Trickster

On this train
I have a box
containing
the 3 beards
and 15 moustaches
I have hidden behind
in my hitherto adult life.

Shortly I will
alight at a town
I have never visited before
where no-one knows me
and begin a new adventure
ignoring the itchiness
of my upper lip.

DAVID ASHFORD

This poem is loosely modelled on an elegy by the seventh-century poetess Al-Khansa, an early convert to Islam, and reputedly Mohammed's favourite poet. Her "Ritha Shakir" is (characteristically) a "refusal to mourn".

Ritha Shakir

Past night to hack out bulimic this swill of bird-song
Put finger to skull and squeeze near total burn-out.
But war is the work sunk deep in the day a blade slung
To strike upon sleeping slow up the throat and pressed hard.
The mouth is apart and purple a taut bikini.

In air pending low scud porn stutter Who Is Conquest
From out of such dawn to focus a point of black light.
Now surge to an eye on rotary wing and snort blood
Lip move about there to clean the confusion Keep Still.
Remote reassembled Spring is on loop it's TV.

If mere utter lying tongue muzzle talk but You're Not
If mere utter lying tongue me that who can withstand.
This word is a green felspar tell of ancient impact
Put flux into heat crush though is a gloss on these raw.
Let eye settle down on gleet suffer child to speak out.

Shakir listen shall I forget cut holes from My World
It's over in stone you roll on a curve in Space-Time.
This rising of sun your photograph you a dead child
But radiant told yr name to the Prophet What's Left.
Can hurt ever come to you never me then That's All.

DAVID COOKE

Paris

Back again in Paris for the first time
in years, I am speaking French to waiters
who bring each morning *café crème*
and a skimpily buttered *sandwich jambon.*

How little seems to have changed
since my fugue in seventy-two –
with too many people smoking
too much and girls cool as mannequins.

I was eighteen, cold, and lapsing slowly,
waiting for someone to find me a job.
My days a chain of vague subjunctives,
I fine-tuned my grammar

at the *Alliance Francaise,* locked out
until the evening from the room I shared
in a hostel with a Senegalese.
He liked to call me *Monsieur David*

but woke me up too early with singsong
prayers I'd never heard before.
Kneeling down on his towel for a mat,
he was paying his dues to Allah,

while my God had wandered off
to a wilderness glimpsed in the prose
of Sartre, or the neverending byways
of Beckett's stumbling purgatory.

An Anniversary

Famous only for Rousseau's dreamy sojourn,
Chambéry lay huddled at the foot
of its calendar landscape, and there it was
we met, as if compelled
by a pattern in the lines on a map
to inhabit that region of mountains.

I wonder now do you still recall
our romantic isolation; how we grew familiar
with narrow streets so reticent and formal,
kept tidy as their own concerns;
cramped shops replete with goods
for a bustling clientele.

All that legendary summer we spent
our afternoons on the slopes
of St. Michel, making love
in a shimmering absence –
with only the insects adrift in silence,
and the gliders above at a decent height.

Travelling Back

I take a train and put your face
behind me, settling back into rhythm
as smartly the wheels gain speed,
then haul across the counties.

And not wanting to read, I try
until suddenly distracted –
my own intangible features
afloat like a wraith in glass

beyond which dissolving
fields becomes a haunt
for predators, a world of tiny
imperceptible shrieks…

Above the merging crowns
of trees this evening's light is wasting.
Pawning our time,
again I'll make it pay.

ED PARSHOTAM

No Dream Is Too Big

Some people believe that no dream is too big.

Other people don't dream they blow smoke rings and cling to a spliff

Hoping the roach can bring them freedom to live

Chocking on dope seems the smokescreen they need for a bit

So they don't notice the things that don't give them reason to grin

Some hit sloe gin till they go pink and think with their fists

And don't dream 'cos when they go sleep their soul leaves and sinks to abyss

The lonely don't believe there's a goal to reach and don't cling to a wish

Won't be going to their knees and won't be seen trying to plead for a lift

Broken relationships, people feel like they don't have a reason to live

They dreamt it would last forever, and now they think that dreaming is shit

I dream my sister's not thinking this now, but a part of me thinks that she is

The clouds aren't seeming to shift

Downhearted feeling adrift

But 'low starting to sink cos I'll swim

No matter how hard beating it is

I think I'll dream for a bit.

ALEX DE SUYS

In Search Of A Theme

(Riffing on the "Pop Up Poetry" Weathervane Poster)

Last time it was "jump the flowers"
But I wasn't ready.
I was a bit confused.
I went and learned how to hit people instead
(In a relaxed and friendly mixed setting)
So the flowers weren't jumped,
Merely trampled
With talk of an alternative venue looking for a host
Only petals in the wind.
Sonofabit*h!
And then no bugger came to my quiz either.
What a cock up!
And as I phone Donall,
Looking for a theme on which to hang my hat
There is only a weird electronic warble
Never before encountered.
So...
Facebook then.
Fu*k me! Chris is featuring!
Theme, theme, theme...

You Don't Need A Weathervane To Tell Which Way The Wind Is Blowing

I wear wind socks.
They're very comfortable
And quite handy if I'm flying a light plane.
"Look at my socks," I say.
"It looks like at least thirty knots blowing in from the West."
Thank god I'm not wearing flares.

Whether

Whether the weather is good or whatever
It's a temperate reason to chat.
Out by the equator.
"It's hot. See you later."
And that, my friends, is that.

Like a Feather in a Gale

Barely do I settle
Than I'm flung off into the maelstrom
Up? Down? Left? Right?
I don't know.
I'm not controlling this ride,
I'm just waiting to see where I end up.
And I think,
This isn't very grown up.
Why don't I take control?
And stop wearing these bloody wind socks.

ERNIE BURNS

Real

It...Is...NOT...real
It must be said
Repeated
This is not real
As the knife goes in
Into the
Seams on reams of paper
Thin forearm skin
Bleeds on black and white
Bleeds on
In libraries and files

This is real
Not understood

Real
Not filled with meaning

And you learn eventually
You have to say to yourself
keep on
Keep on saying
This is NOT real

A New Poem By Ernie Burns

The problem, if there is a problem
And there is a fucking problem
When seen In the cold hard light of the glamorous spotlight
The "so called" problem is...

and

Whilst It can be mis-seen easily
During the dancing little jigs

or

If riding
On real horses
Pretending a life wholly natural
The grooms following brandishing shovels

"Oh, how delightful! There will be a ball after all
It will be covered in all the pest periodicals
I meant to say "best", dreary me"
(To be read in a mock worthy accent)
(Everything in brackets iterated)

The refrain, a terrible well trodden Cliché
Ricocheting from lip to lip
Frankly with so little self awareness
It is fucking scary
It should be called "The Journalist's Twist"
That light jazz motif to play at soirees
That refrain is giving class a bad reputation
With those fuck you beats
And off melody

Back to the problem
And It is, that we believe there to be a solution
When there isn't even a question
How stupid!

DONALL DEMPSEY

Blue Dress

(for Junie)

We sit
in an enormous field

that greens
around us

your blue dress

nailing us to
the centre of the universe

you making me
jewellery

from bright young daises

as I breathe softly
upon a dandelion clock

and time
holding forever it's breath

forever holding

your laughing
beautiful face

smiling through the dancing
dandelion seeds

as I smile
years later

through my tears.

Singing The River

Walking with my uncle was never
the ordinary process of perambulation.

in order to get from pt. A to
pt. Z.

We would sing our way west into
the field as if to

tame it
soothe it with sound.

"On Carrigdhoun the heath is brown..."
we'd sing to it

"...the clouds are dark o'er Ard-na-Lee."

The grass listening with its thousand ears.

And the field would swoon
and fall down

to the river at its border
(which as it happened

was the real life river
of the song)

"...to kiss the slumbering Own na Buidhe."

As if we had sung it
into existence.

And we would roll ourselves down
over and over until

we arrived at its dizzy waters
dangling our toes

in pure song.

And now (with a quick uncle wink)
"Let's walk home....backwards!"

And backwards home we'd go
just for the laugh of it.

The yes of it!

Confusing cows
and a few scattered clouds.

Trees and hedges tiptoeing
away from us.

The five-bar gate with
the sweetest wildest strawberries at its feet

proclaiming: "Is it mad...
...y'are or....wot?"

And the next day off we'd go walking eyes closed
in a darkness of our own making

to sing its song
to the river

the river chuckling
over stones to itself.

And the next next day would be
backwards with eyes closed

led along by our own laughter
and the odd mystified moo.

"Farewell..." we'd tell
the sleepy river "...farewell!"

leaving it dreaming
in a sunset.

"Shhhhhh..." shushed our footsteps
shhhhhhs walking backwards,

"When Donal swore, aye o'er and o'er,
We'd part no more a stór mo chroidhe."

"shhhhhhhhhhhh.....shhhhhhhhhhhh!"
"shhhhhhhhhhhh.....shhhhhhhhhhhh!"

"....shhhhhhhhhhhh!"

LOUISE ETHERIDGE

Ballet Boyz In The Theatre

Ballet Boyz in the theatre.
Bare chests
And lean, muscular arms
And wiry dancer physiques.
In your flesh-coloured tights
It looks like you are dancing naked.
That's worth the price of a front row seat.

It's so nice to see men dancing *together.*
They dance vulnerability and grace
And all the things women are allowed to be, all the time.
They dance power, strength and teamwork
And all the things women might like to be shown doing more of.
To be honest, I've got to fix that sentence.

My gaze is 40% amazement, 30% appreciation and 30% ogling.
I rather like the Italian one.
I will stare at him.
And stare. And stare.
Oh, he's noticed. I've unnerved him. He's fallen.
I should probably take my balaclava *off.*

Boobs

My boobs have never been what you call big;
Unlike my friend Julie's; she paid for her rig.
They were massive and ripe, a triple F cup,
She looked like Mae West but she couldn’t stand up.
She kept tipping over, with frightful abandon;
At least her big boobs gave her something to land on.
But she was persuasive; she told me I'd be
Much less of a woman, without surgery.

I went to the surgeon, the signs I misread,
“What's that bulge in your pants?” " It's my wallet" he said.
"I'll slice and I'll dice your pathetic wee boobs,
Then I'll drill and I'll fill them with old inner tubes,
Then I’ll pump them with silicon, formed into rounds,
Then I’ll charge you the fee which is ten thousand pounds.
Nipples are extra, one lump or two?"
I made my excuses and cried in the loo.

I mused on the issue and, even if wealthy,
There's no way I'd fuck up my boobs, 'cos they're healthy.
They do the job well, they fill up a bra,
Blokes say that they're lovely; they're fine how they are.

So what if you lie down and witness your tits
Slop sideways and backwards down into your pits?
So what if they're weeny, a pair of fried eggs
Popped out by the teeniest hen on two legs?
You can be confident they won't explode
On economy seats on the way back from Rhodes,
You can be certain that each time you sneeze
Those silicon bastards won't shoot round your knees.

So, when you see boobs with a person attached
and you know that your own ones are very mismatched,
Stick your hand down your bra for a bit of a feel,
Your tits might be weird but at least they are real.

MARIAN FIELDING

Not Me

Outside the greengrocer's the other day
a stranger holding a single red rose
smiled and advanced in my direction.

It was like that advertisement for specs,
where the girl running towards her lover stops
and kisses the old guy just in front of him.

The man with the flower wasn't good-looking,
in fact he was rather dumpy. But when he marched right past
I was surprised to feel my solar plexus plummet.

Suddenly, there I was, thirteen years old again,
pale blue Alice band thrust through back-combed hair
being chatted up by a boy at my new youth club.

The next week I went back, he waved across the room
and I responded, heart hammering.
You already know what happened.

The Pea

Dear Mum,
I don't know how it happened -
I made the bed
the way you taught me,
meticulous to the point of perfect symmetry,
smoothed the silk sheets
calmed the wrinkles with my palm
honed hospital corners straight as glass -
a treat for the tenderest arse.

No one's ever complained before.
So how did it happen?
I say that so-called princess, lady la de da
must have invented it, lock, stock and leguminous barrel.
Marriage was on her agenda
and that's what I told my employer,
but he took offence
and now I'll never get a decent reference.
Love Brenda

Dear B,
Am so sorry, but don't worry,
I've got you a job!
The seven dwarves next door,
tell me they're desperately short of a cleaner
since their last one ran off
with some toff.
Love
Mum

PETER FISHER

Dusty Tears

The tracks of tears on dusty cheeks that fell from the eyes that were dulled by a vision of tomorrow.
The head held high in defiance of a fate that could not be worse than what had gone before.
The blood-soaked shirt that hung from the wire like a flag from a long forgotten cause.
This is the price of your lie.

The distended belly, the sunken eyes, the silence in the midst of so much pain.
The standing in line without expectation of ever tasting the prize.
The unspoken sorrow of the dignified heart just waiting for the end.
This is the price of your lie.

And now the walls that once surrounded your deceit and held you safe are slowly crumbling.
And the detachment of your soul from the actions of your hand will crush your heart.
And the values that you touted and never practiced are now rampaging at your door.
And still you cling to your lie.

NEIL FLATMAN

New For Old

Unlike the roar of its predecessor
strafing like a jet through the old-school
coffee shop, the new machine
extrudes reluctant steam with a dull hum.

My companion spoons clouds from his cappuccino:
all foam thunderheads and chocolate snow,
shows me pictures of his bonus wife,
the Winston Churchill baby, absent cigar
and his new silver Porsche, just like the last.

We talk about about his sons at university
to whom he speaks and his ex
to whom he never does
as coffee drips unnoticed on his red silk tie,
blood from a wound.

We've been coming here for twenty years,
to unpack the bones and shells of men
shake them gently, read the signs
while sunlight reflects off the vinyl-tops
which still and always lurch without a wedge
but the coffee never tastes the way it smells
no matter the machine.

CATHY FLOWER
pfl (Poet for Life)

The Next Morning

Too many reds
No bread
You were off your head
Don't you know by now
That the hatch you fill
Is to be your kill?
(Dank is your quill)

You should know by now

Independence was your motto
Your style is cramped?
Make room
Know no strife
You know it well
No strife (*pause*)

You little corpse
Get it right

All the church bells chime…
All the sirens shriek …
Every pane, every glass in every colour
Shape or form smashes…

Don't worry
These are just stanza of words
One million hands clap in sync…
Wild wind swept waves crash on every coastline…
Every wolf howls…
Every naked metal coat hanger falls off every
Clothes rack, landing on every hard floor known

The global asylums of drummers bang on - and on - and on…
All the dragsters fire up their engines before they
Scream down an endless raceway
In unison, multiple space shuttles launch
Amplification deafens…

Be strong

Be cashmere

Don't get it wrong.

Blue Poetry **by Cathy Flower**

ROBERT GARNHAM

Poem

This is a poem about bubbles.
I wanted it to be about coat hangers.
But it's about bubbles.
Bubbles are round and they float up
And then down and often they pop.
Coat hangers don't do either of those things.

Bubbles are transient and they do not live forever.
They teach us that nothing lasts.
Mind you neither do coat hangers these days.
I bought some from Poundstretcher and one of them snapped.
Bubbles float on the breeze and they reflect the sun.
In rainbow hues resplendent oily iridescent pearlescent luminescent
fluttery fluttery pop pop
In a way that coat hangers can never replicate.

You can't hang your jacket on a bubble.
You can't wedge a wardrobe door open with a bubble.
You can't use a bubble for a car aerial on a 1985 Ford Sierra.
You can't scratch your back with a bubble.
You can't get a chocolate digestive out from under the fridge with a bubble.
You can't have a coat hanger bath.
You can't hook bubbles over the metal bar in your wardrobe.

Poem

I always seem to associate
Several Surrey towns
With shades of beige as marketed
By the Ford Motor Company in the 1970s.

Egham is Nevada beige.
Woking is Sahara beige.
Weybridge is classic cream beige.
Guildford is light beige.
Staines is antique beige.

I know Staines has a Middlesex postal address
But it's definitely in Surrey.

My friend Steven opines
That I always get excitable
And blunder on through life
And he might have a point.

I like the display of busts
In one of the galleries at the British Museum.
I can't remember which gallery it is
But they've all got big sideburns
And the sun slants oblong like solid dust.
I put my hand in the dust slant solid beam.

Haslemere is Bahama beige.
Horsell is Toucan beige.
Bracknell is in Berkshire but it's milk caramel beige.

In 1995 I had a bad cycle accident
And my nose has been this shape ever since.

I fell off my bike in Englefield Green
(Sonic beige)

Went riiiiiiiiiight over the handlebars.

I take time now and then
To slow down and savour life
And to commune with the exact platzgeist
Of a place / moment.

So up yours, Steven.
See, I can do it sometimes.

At nights the trains used to spark electric and
Light up the skies,
Silhouetting
Holloway College like Dracula's Castle.
And I'd get ever so scared
Until,
Lulled to sleep by the friendly roar
Of transcontinental jets,
I'd dream of labyrinthine holiday cottages.

ANDY V FROST

Aftermath

The approach to Morden is spattered
with random splurges
of twisted metal and torn fabric
drowning in puddles.

Further in,
the Station and unwitting epicentre
of this Umbrella Graveyard
is unmoved amidst the annihilation.

On Mitcham Common,
a few trees are down
but most stand firm,
their positions held and secure.

The roads and the kerbs though,
are littered with fractured twigs
and the last leaves of autumn.
Collateral damage of capricious gusts

Croydon is a Maelstrom;
hordes of modern-day hunters seeking
the ultimate prize to allow escape
from this mad melee

The full extent of the storm damage
will only be visible
once the shop doors are locked
and the Christmas shoppers have departed.

Stan

He opened the shed door with a grin,
pulled back a tarpaulin to reveal
antique metal of serious purpose.

Reaching for a rag,
he bunched and stuffed it into
the gaping bell-mouth.

"No choke" he said
as he flicked levers marked prime and advance,
twisting another, ninety degrees.

Shifting his balance,
he felt his way to Before-Top-Dead-Centre
and lunged with full weight on the kickstart.

Promising splutters saw five minutes of repeat
for a slow-beat cacophony played
through a fishtail cornet.

The grin was now mutual, Bikers unite!
Though this barking beast
was older than my father.

He shut it off to talk.
Admired my bike and its ease of starting
on freezing mornings.

He told me things before I asked them,
was shocked at how fast and reliable
my little Yamaha was.

Two Petrol-heads, a generation apart.
One revving up to Williams
One ruminating, on when Ixion was the Word.

MARK GILFILLAN (The Stokey Bard)

A Time Of Introspection

She walks amid
aged crooked stones
her dreams fall silent
as a new fall snow
hopes and fears
float as myriad spores
carried away
upon a light
and whispered
summer breeze
a time of introspection

five haiku

i took a picture
six sharp pencils for my task
joining up the stars

two ropes and a board
swings across the universe
clutching out at stars

a splash of scarlet
on a white canvas of snow
a robin visits

a wooden park bench
steeples pierce a gauloise mist
peaceful points of view

forget the mundane
climb a ladder to the moon
tell me what you see

Slipping Through The Gears

slipping through the gears
i round the slow sweeping curve of the river bank
and out to a necklace of house boats
stretched out painted, half asleep
at this point the towpath
seems to stretch on forever
slipping through the gears
i slalom around the dog walkers
and lazy lovers
pinging my bell
just to let them know I'm here…….i'm near
up to the north
an industrial line of pylons
legs akimbo
alien robot invaders
striding across lush golden fields
cycling on past
lock after lock after lock
to where the river calms
to a deep green reedy slowness
or clarity of stillness
here
weeping willows
dip their toes
as the odd kayak drifts on by
time to turn and head for home
……..slipping through the gears

GRAHAM GODDARD
aka Oh Standfast

Judge's Notes

She took me on a journey all the way back
From the time of Doncaster boogie and Luxembourg rap

She was marvellous, disastrous,
She needed plumber & plasterers

She was Morgan Freeman, Kevin Keegan, Martin Sheen
& Steve McQueen

And the great escape is what I was needing
Cos after ten minutes my ears were bleeding

She was a sweet-savoury fusion
A menu-abroad confusion

She was Edgar, she was Allen, She was Poe
She was Dot, she was Ian, she was Phil, Pat & Mo.

She couldn't sing for toffee and I loved that fact
The last thing she needs is more sweets & that

She'd be dragged out at Christmas like
Monopoly, Sudoku, Scrabble, Kerplunk!

The NME would describe her as
Screamo-Hardcore-Folk-Disc-Donk-Funk!

She's a two fingered salute hiatus
To the inevitable D-list celebrity status

And What Do You Do?

I am an internationally acclaimed professor of sport
I work for the Royal Mail, I sort.
I am an optician specialising in those with eyesight that is short.
In the nineteen nineties I taught… media.

I am a cheerleader
An infamous arts dealer
A west highland terrier dog breeder
I am the owner of a pop up coffee shop in Brighton called
'Quadrocaffeinia'

I am on a gap year.
I am still on a gap year.

I am freelance chiropodist
A struck off dentist
I am a classical pop funk fusion Cellist
I work in a florist… on Sunday.

I am training to be an astronaut and I hope to orbit the Earth one day.

You know the star signs in the back of papers, I draw those little pictures.
See those kitchen cabinets, I mould the fixtures.

I am a dustbin lorry driver
An ex Special Forces deep sea diver
I live off royalties from back when I penned the U2 hit 'Desire'.
I am an inherent liar.

But that's enough about me.

And what do you do?

Life Sized Model

I've got a life sized model of Dame Judi Dench
In a World War II scenario digging out a trench
Her face is more screwed up than normal due to the stench
Oh I've got a life sized model of Dame Judi Dench.

I've got a life sized model of Justin Bieber
His head has been severed by a rusty meat cleaver
Due to the fact I'm not a Justin believer
Oh I've got a life sized model of Justin Bieber,

Graham Goddard

You insisted on the window seat

You fell asleep within

45 seconds

You woke up 4500

miles later.

Don't talk to me.

GRIM CHIP

Not Wisely

It isn't easy, getting any credit nowadays.
Who's going to trust you with their money,
Or their heart? And there is not much love
Available to anyone, even for those who try
Their best, who do their bit, who play their part,
Who step up when it's going down. But,
If you're made that way, then that's the way you're made.

So maybe virtue is its own reward,
There are no accolades, there's little praise,
And it's a crown of thorns that's worn
By anyone who cares too much.
Life's such a bitch but it's the dark clouds
Make the silver lining shine
And who would want it any other way?

Plenty! Or so it seems and so they say
That they already live in paradise,
We know that we will never reach the promised land,
Though we can walk a step or two together,
Shoulder to shoulder,
Heart to heart,
And hand in hand.

Packaway

Pack away the nurseries into a soundbite,
Close hospitals, turn fire-stations into luxury flats.
The city alchemists have done their best
To kill the goose that laid the golden egg
But that's the beauty of it;
Base metal from the common weal can still be conjured with.
A mark is stamped upon the penny-post
And pennies pinched from public-sector plebs
Will reap a handsome dividend.

Deliberate denigration softens up the target,
Undermines educators,
Healers, helpers, first responders,
Are parcelled-up, and privatised.
Infants in incubators, undergraduates,
Infirm incontinents in care homes,
Are carried off by speculators
Unencumbered by the smallest moral compass.
The profit margin is their only friend.

So pack away the nursery, the books, the toys,
The instruments of learning and of fun,
Pack up the little girls and boys into
An education system sabotaged
And broken, quite undone
By petty dogma, self-interest and greed.
Don’t say that you weren’t warned.
Unpack the future for them,
Strange and dark, indeed.

The Anti-Saccharites

We lived off the fat of the land for years.
Much good it did us, clogged our arteries and drained our souls.
Hard times a-come and life is not as sweet as once it was:
The gravy train, the trail of tears; the silver spoons,
The begging bowls. But just because

You're worth it, don't mean you'll get what we deserve:
The striver or the shirker; rich or poor.
Trickle-down slows, flows like treacle or molasses.
Say what? They've got a nerve to tell us less is more,
And syrup-coated words from members of the upper classes

Take the biscuit. It's hard to swallow bullshit, or austerity
When our prosperity was built on other's pain.They'd have
Their cake and eat it, then and now; equality be damned!
The ocean had three sides to it, and sugar is a demon once again;
The Anti-Saccharites would understand.

But there are other imports; reggae, rum, and rude bwoy style
To re-invent the nation. A little lime might cure
Those scurvy knaves who just won't think it through.
A brown-skinned blue-eyed honey makes me smile;
Take your licks in real time; how do you want it, one lump or two?

SUE GUINEY

Home Stay

She calls me 'Sues'
turning my name into something Khmer
complete with its random final 's'.
As young as my youngest, she takes care of me.
Sues, brush your teeth she laughs just after dinner.
Sues, put bones here she cautions, removing those bones
she permits herself to eat.

She teaches me Khmer as I teach her English.
We communicate with more than words.
She shows me how to fan myself,
how to wash my knickers in her round black tub.
I squat beside it as she pours water in
from the large stone jar. Rain water into plastic,
rinse it twice then hang.

She has given me more than a place to stay.
She has taught me an old way to live,
reminded me of all I can do without, and all
that I can't.

A generation, a world, an economy apart
makes no difference now. We are friends.
Srey Mom, *girl mom* –
she has been all that to me.
Now when I brush my teeth at night, I'll
think of her and smile.

My Water Bottle

Its frosted glass feels cold, as frosted things should,
and looks cloudy, hiding whatever is inside
as if a secret -- pillow talk
hinted at within a parched night.

The water is cold, at most times.
I reach for it at odd hours.
Quietly it reminds me to be thankful
that my nighttime fears are unfounded.

Even in the dark, its curves can be sensed.
The moonlight from the haphazardly dropped shade
illuminates the wide hips, the slender neck, the body
pricked by dainty blue raised hand-painted flowers.

But the glass isn't clear and when I reach for it
I'm no longer clear myself, just a shadow
of an outline of a hand outstretched in need.

Funny how things change with the night.
Early, when its neighbor, the lamp, knows it's time to go dark,
the water bottle sits in Victorian purposefulness,
just beautiful enough, but really there for a reason: to do its duty
for my reaching hand and dry throat.

But later, sometime before dawn, its form is forgotten and it sits
by my bed, as seriously as a night nurse ready to work,
to ease the pain of that arid dream, to lubricate, resuscitate
as if into a starched white, curtain-shielded bed.

At dawn, it watches me rise from flooded midnight.
The glass still frosted and cold, but more distinct now.
The water within less cold, but still quenching.
It sits and keeps waiting. Despite whatever state
it may find me, it remains there to help, without judgment,
to be reached for and found full.

Mekong Woman

She opens shop along its muddy shore.
   Mango, two dollah. You want?
Sparse teeth.
Dirty nails.
Twisted hair still gleaming black.

Another walks with a French posture,
her head is taller than the length of her back. Her arms
are hooked around her sister's.
   Bonsoir, Monsieur. Merci. Orgoon.

Luring men in by downcast eyes, demure
beneath midnight black lashes. Flashes
of cold escape from their eyes.
The thrust of the river propels.

There is beauty in their duplicity.
There is honour in their slim advantage.

The men slip sleepy heads from *tuk tuk* seats.
The men sleep for us all. It's their right to do nothing.
It's our duty to do the rest.

Power lies in unexploded bombs.

JENNIFER A MCGOWAN

Bearing Witness

What kind of a man
ties himself to the mast
without even a knife in his boot?
It was three hours later
that we noticed him signalling;
halfway to Scylla and Charybdis
before we untied him.
We enjoy a laugh, after all.

It's all very well weaning yourself
off opium, lotus, whatever,
but when your reward
is to tie yourself
to the underside of a fucking sheep—
well, there are sheep at home,
that's all I'll say.
And pigs. Pigs!
Not a one of us got a look-in
while he, the big O,
screwed Circe's brains out.
So good he just had to go back.
"So sorry your mum died,"
she said the second time, cooing,
those big deer eyes, long legs,
pulling him back down on the bed.
We knew whose wand had the pulling power,
but Odysseus had a thing
about size, not skill. Holy moly.

So, yeah, we knew the signs.
Ten-year contract with over seven years left;
no sign of Ithaca. Not good odds.

And damn, we were hungry
after a year of acorns.
Six hundred cattle!
We fancied a steak.
Oh, he told us “no,”
but you know, after the trip out,
the whole war, the flesh-eaters,
the singing birds—there’s only
so much “no” you can take.

We were shipwrecked, of course.
Only one survivor.
And Odysseus, free of us,
fell on his feet, another dame-with-a-C,
Calypso. Seven years there,
and then a princess!
While we
wait at this ditch
for a hint of blood.
Bastard.

Vade Mecum

I carry you with me
like a bruise:
dark, tender, incompletely hidden.

Loneliness is a secretive art.
It can be flaunted,
but in the open, discussed calmly
over tea, it becomes
something other than itself—
a badge of pride, a medal
cast from the pain
that bore it.

The hat you left,
a tatty bookmark, an umbrella
rattling in its stand.
These are my manuals
for remembering your touch,
your voice, the way
you giggled at mirrors,
how you liked music loud.
With each passing day
I sing your name more slowly,
a hesitant litany, a half-remembered prayer,
like a rosary dropped at the station
waiting for the final tread.

ROYA HAMID

Words Worth

There are words that I like that I never get to use
Like flummox, oleaginous and bumbling and ruse
Does there need to be meaning in the words that I choose
Or can I put any words together for all to peruse?

Patty, globule, drizzle and chunk
I like the sound of these bad boys: isthmus and flunk
Is isthmus near to Christmas in sound only and not meaning
And what about fair dinkum and blaspheming
And what about protuberance and tolerance and prance
The sound of all these words have got me in a trance

I don't care about much for content, depth or reason
I'd rather say rotund, presumptuous and phonetician
Get your mouth, tongue and ears in a flap
With words like milimology and gruesome synap.

With a rinky dinky doodle rolling round your tongue
And an organic stickaboo emanating from the lung
I would rather not be overly dependent on rationale and reason
The intellect I do detect is truly so last season

GARY W HARTLEY
(Gary From Leeds)

Crisis Consumer

When Woolworths needed me
I was there on the front line
Filling plural basket
With pick 'n mix
Mainly pink shrimps
It didn't work, though

When Virgin Megastore
Became Zavvi
Became even more screwed
I bought all the Top 40
On all formats available
It didn't work, though

When Bear Stearns
Started to keel over
I got approved for
A sub-prime mortgage
With all the trimmings
Including a mini-jacuzzi
In the back yard
It didn't work, though

Today, Morrisons
I am here for you
Buying a pint of semi-skimmed
And 18 multi-packs of Discos
And I'm asking you
To just ignore precedents
Because I know you'd
Do the same for me.

Strangers In A Home

Burglar don't like their Hitchcock
Rifled through the box set
Not one to their taste

Vertigo's avoidance
Predictable given
Their ground-floor entry

But judging by the scuff-marks
You'd have assumed an interest
In *Rear Window* at least

They took a half-finished
Bottle of Robinson's squash
A bag of Haribo

But steered well clear
Of *Frenzy, Rope*
And even *Psycho*

Burglar don't like their Hitchcock
Is this non-theft a critique?

An attack on the Hackneyed dialogue
Of *The Birds*
The overuse of concluding
Action sequences in music halls

Or Alfred's output being
Far sketchier generally than
Self-described film-buffs attest

Or maybe it's just
A simple show of disapproval
At this 14-disc set's omission
Of *North by Northwest*

JANIS HAVES

PRINT MEANS CAPITALS

PRINT MEANS CAPITALS, BLACK PEN, FULL NAME
TIGHT INSIDE THE YELLOW BOX, CROSSING OUT
VOIDS CLAIM
FILES TOWERING PIZZA HIGH – TOTAL FAILURE TO
COMPLY
GO TO SECTION 14A THEN SIT AND HAVE A GOOD CRY

MY ADMINISTRATIVE EFFORTS HAVE BEEN DESCRIBED AS
NEGLIGENT
I THINK THAT I WAS BORN WITH AN EFFICIENCY
IMPEDIMENT
THE PROBLEM'S ROOTED IN A LACK OF MOTIVATION TO
BEGIN
MY HEAD STARTS SPINNING FASTER THAN THE GHOST OF
ANNE BOLEYN
THAT DOCUMENT YOU'RE LOOKING FOR GOT FILED IN
THE BIN
I GUESS I SHOULD HAVE FILLED IN THAT REQUEST FOR
NEXT OF KIN

I KNOW THAT I PROCRASTINATE WHEN THERE IS DATA
TO COLLATE
THERE IS NO PILE, NO PAST DUE DATE THAT I CAN'T
CIRCUMNAVIGATE

CATEGORISE, ALPHABETISE – DO THEY HAVE THAT IN A
    LARGER SIZE?
I'M EASILY DISTRACTED WHEN THE FILING IS PROTRACTED

DON'T TIE ME UP IN RED TAPE
THWART MY VAIN ATTEMPTS AT ESCAPE
THIS PHOBIA OF FILING COULD BE FATAL WHEN COMPILING
THE TRANSFERENCE OF DATA TO A SPREADSHEET
    THREE MILES LONG
YOU'VE NO IDEA HOW MANY WAYS I FIND TO GET IT
    WRONG
MY CROSSINGS OUT ARE LEGENDARY
MY ATTENTION SPAN IS TEMPORARY
TO THE GODS OF ADMINISTRATION
I PRAY FOR MY LIBERATION

NUMBER CRUNCHERS, WORK THROUGH LUNCHERS
HOBNOB ON YOUR TEABREAK MUNCHERS
I APPEAL TO YOU IN TRIPLICATE TO SAVE ME FROM MY
    PLIGHT
STILL THE SHREDDER WORKS QUITE NICELY

I THINK IT IS PRECISELY
THE SOLUTION I'VE BEEN LOOKING FOR
WITH THAT I'LL SAY GOODNIGHT

A F HARROLD

The Poet Mends A Tap

Then I put down the spanner
and unwind the tap by hand,
rip the old washer out with pinch-nosed pliers,
squeeze the fresh dry one down
onto the nodule in the middle
of this heavy cold machined metal lump.

And now the bath no longer drips,
not even when I've turned the stopcock
and heard the rattling chug
as water pushes air out of the pipes.

You're away and it's a Sunday morning.
The cat's in the garden,
out chasing flies or grass or lying down asleep
beneath the thorny brambles somewhere cool.

And the house is too quiet without the drip,
the sunlight too clear.

I lift the spanner, spin its adjustable wheel,
heft its weight it in my hand
and wonder just how easy or how hard it would be
to undo all the good I've done.

Jackdaw

Head bald as a vulture's head,
body thin-feathered, ill-looking,
scrawny as a chicken in the freezer,
but with wings night-black,

thick and full of flight,
this young jackdaw negotiates the feeder,
wheedles out its chunk of cheese,
crumps to the lawn, turns it, spins it,
swallows it.

Pigeons crowd it, bully it like pigeons,
but mother sits beside it,
lets it make its own way.
Coal-dust wings and ancient pate,
wizened before its age.

The robin flutters to the fence,
takes one look at this thing
and scarpers to a different garden entirely.

Struck

Imagine life without its soundtrack.
Even train journeys would be dull
in a world bare of rhythmic pulses.

And not just music lost from speakers,
pianos struck dumb in the corners,
guitars gathering dust in concert halls,

but also the thunderstorm impotent
above the city, looming apologetically,
all those empty-throated showers at dawn,

and up in the trees silent birds, hopeful
that someone will notice their plumage,
will flit over, wanting to chat them up.

Cat Above Pigeons

The neighbours made their first mistake
by shoring up the wooden frame;
their second by unrolling chicken wire;
and their third in filling it with doves.

An aviary, in the garden next door?
A box of feathers the other side of the fence?
We hardly see our cat these days:

he's discovered the joys of television.

He sits there for hours, chin chittering
at all the things he sees that'll never be his.
Pigeons flap anxious, embarrassed.

He can't understand why they're not free,
why they don't come to him when he calls.

The world's unfair in so many different ways.

Found Poem

So, Kurt Vonnegut, in his short novel *Cat's Cradle*,
has a character characterise humans as being mud,
but mud, importantly, that got the chance to sit up
and look around. There is a disaster. Everyone dies.

There is a disaster in the real world too. We all die.
I simply wanted to remind myself of what he says,
of how I should feel lucky for having had all of this.
After all, I got so much, and most mud got so little.

FRAN ISHERWOOD

Anne Of Grey Gables

"What a grey day!" as Larry Grayson could have said.
Grayish graveyard grey, though urban logical rather
than country elegiacal. A dead dove in pigeon's clothing.
Sheepish clouds blend in by disguising themselves
as drear smears and smudges on dirty spectacles.
Don't look at me! Be still my bleating heart.
A block of flats that shines seaside white on summer's day
now clad in a lighter shade of stale, morosely regards
the sky. They collude as a paint shop card chart of taster daubs
for the less adventurous person. This is a day, not elephant grey
but paler .Whither the sailor's trousers run up by the sky tailor?
The drama of storms & gales has now gone to reveal lacklustre
firmament portraying the hollowness in between grief
and moving on, Limbo amid negativity and positivity.

Two months on from the unseasonably sunny day
that became the night he left us, and the ensuing
dark days & nights when undecorated trees, dragged
flicking & screaming by angry tempest, rapped impatiently
at the living room window to be let in out of the deluge.
Jealous of the ostensibly cosy Christmas scene of
family trying to carry on with the occasion that Dad loved,
the trees were wistfully unaware of care to fill the empty chair.
Grief has, for today, reinvented itself as homelyapathy.
Futility has flounced in sulkily, swishing her long skirt.
I consider phoning my Mum to see how she is doing
I don't want to infect her with my nothingness.
No wit. No blandishments. Just bland on Blonde.
No hope, no spring, no crocus, and no focus.

Eurovision Song Contest 2003

Two days before: The departure lounge is Faithful -full
with gaggles of excited, gay men, skeins of middle aged
female pilgrims wearing glitter embossed union jack t-shirts
and a boodle of bald blokes, bags full of Duty-Free booty.

I want to tell them: My brother wrote the UK song!
I don't. No-one speaks to me. The chatter, sprinkled
with the odd spurt of singing continues throughout
the flight. As we land in Riga, applause erupts.

The night before: My sisters and I, and a smattering
of others, in a vast stadium, watch five hours or so
of dress rehearsal. Despite boredom superseding
novelty, nobody sings out of tune. All monitors function.

The Night: We are warned to sit low in our front row seats
to avoid a camera that swings precariously above our heads.
The British act sounds fine to us but as the results come in
we will cringewrithe to sink lower and lower in our seats.

I imagine how my brother, watching on a big screen
in Albert Square, Manchester, with a host of local VIPs
and a hitherto proud Home crowd, might feel right now,
probably,"Infamy, Infamy! They've all got it in for me!"

"Le Royaume-Uni: Nul point". "Velika Britanija :Nul point"
"Den brittiska:No points." At the backstage party our duo,
beseiged by paparazzi, battle past, haunted, to leave. I phone
home and am told that my eight year old son has been weeping.

Midnight: It only goes dark for a couple of hours. Forgetting
the zeros by zeroing in on the free bar, we conga with TV crews
and presenters around an indoor fountain then drink fizzy wine
at outside tables till it stays light, at about seven in the morning.

2 days after: At the airport, we show printouts of the deluge
of vile bile upchucked by the British press, to the band's managers.
Chuckling, they say it is the next best thing to winning. Indeed,
my brother will later say that he is crying all the way to the bank.

Mine's A Pint

In a mill town in a monochromatic nation

She was born in between the publication

of Cat In The Hat and Kathy Kirby's first EP.

Her Dad, in a name book, was pleased to see

that Frances meant "Free" and Mary, "Bitter"

thus wetting the head of this first of the litter.

GHAREEB ISKANDER

Darkness

Translated from the Arabic by M T Ali

Nothing,
Except this darkness
Nothing,
Once more white tears will come down on you
Piles of damaged things
Endings, which will flash and disappear

You have nothing in this world
Except for the word
So says the poet

Ascend with it
Ascend to the end of the mountain

The bright mountain of gaiety
Or the dark mountain of the ending

Ascend to the sea,
I don't mean the sea of words
The sea of lies
Or the sea of truths

It's only a sea,
This, which stands
Behind you

Admire its beaches,
Which don't flash
Nor disappear

The beaches of hope
The beaches of spirit,
Which light up
Amidst this darkness

It isn't the beaches of gaiety

It isn't the beaches of the small river,
Which our childhood used to cross

It's the beaches of tears with which
We wrote our poems
On the messy school exercise books

Beaches of blood,
Which used to flow
On the streets of our innocence, which wilted
Our innocence, which still blazes
blazes
bla…

But,
in the end
there is
Nothing
except for
Darkness.

On Loneliness

Translated by Fathieh Saudi and SallyThompson

The sky darkens
whilst you
sitting alone
bite into a withered apple

Darkness doesn't stand for the womb
nor is the apple synonymous with
Adam
not this time…!

It was by chance
just you
sitting alone
biting into a withered apple.

MARTIN JONES

My Brother's Keeper

The other day
I met James Joyce.

I was sitting in a coffee bar
where they pack you in tightly.

There he was beside me
reading a book,
My Brother's Keeper,
the book of recollections
by his brother, Stanislaus.

"Interesting?" I inquired.

He was Irish, he said.
He was an actor, he went on,
studying to play a part
in a film about James Joyce:
his younger self,
his older self,
and his friendship with the tenor,
Count John McCormack.

"And you're his younger self?"

"Yes," he confirmed,
as if to prove the point
showing lean sensitive features
and dark unruly hair.

It was time for me to go.
Various quips rose to mind
none worthy of the occasion.

"Bye," I merely said.

He looked up from his book.

"Bye," he merely said
with haunting Irish voice.

Kate Moss In The Restaurant

There was, I admit,
something special about her.

I found myself looking again,
wondering about her age,
about the sources of her beauty;

wondering, too,
why she'd suddenly entered.

As she at once proclaimed,
it wasn't to eat a meal,
merely to greet the manager.

Much more, so it seemed,
it was to show the little doggies
she cradled in her arms.

Fortunately, among our party,
there was a lovely lady
who was crazy about cats -

a passion she now transferred
to these cute little doggies:
kissed their tiny noses,
murmured unintelligible words.

Kate was delighted.

Meanwhile, in the background,
there lurked a male figure,
boyfriend or bodyguard.

This memory donated,
she joined him in the street.

MEL JONES

Dead Colourful

You peacocked down Camden High Street
Too cool for green
And blue
Only emerald and cobalt
Were good enough for you

They're not clothes
They're statements!
I am a neutron-blonde attack!

A red noose always at your neck
Rose, you insisted
Hovering above
Your lurid stride
And those designer coffee shoes

What colour were the pills you used?
Death by rainbow would be just like you

You promised to haunt me
Pyrotechnically
If you went first into the black
But old shades fade my dear
Ground down
To an indeterminate hue

Customer Service

Good morning, Mel speaking. How may I help you?
I wanna job, Love.
Ok. And what kind of work are you looking for?
Full time.
Yes, but what do you want to do?
Shifts.
And when you are on a shift, what kind of work are you doing?
Whatever I'm told. I'm a very good worker.
I'm sure. But what I'm trying to get at it is what you actually do.
Oh I can turn my hand to most things .
Right. But what do you tend to turn your hand too most of the time?
Well, I'm unemployed at the moment.
I'm sorry to hear that. What would you like to do?
Like I say, get a job.
Which job?
What have you got?
Ok. To help you I need to know a bit about the jobs you've done before.
What was your last job?
I had two jobs.
And what were they?
They were alright as it goes, but I got sacked.
I'm sorry to hear that, but what were you sacked from?
Both of them.
Oh dear. Ok. Let's look at this another way.
Do you have any qualifications?
Oh yes .
And what are they?
I got an NVQ and a City and Guilds.
In what?
College.
Ok. And when you left College, you got a job?
Yes.

And what was your job?
I was an assistant.
Assisting who?
The manager.
Managing what?
Me.
When you were doing what?

Working! Are you thick or something?

I'm seriously beginning to wonder. I still have no idea what you do.
Oh. Didn't I say?
Communications.....

Faster Melly-Mel, Kill Kill!

I thought that it might be cathartic
To list everyone I would kill
If I knew there'd be no consequences
And my conscience had died, or got ill.

I'd start with the usual suspects
The patently evil and bad
But I have an uncomfortable feeling
After that I might go a bit mad.

I'd shoot every Tesco timewaster
Those prats just ahead in the queue
Who pay when they get to the checkout
In pennies........ five-pences......
And twos.

I'd waste anyone with a buggy
You're the one who had kids, dear, not me
And wankers who can't find their ticket -
They'd all cark it on my killing spree.

The boys with their pants round their ankles
The girls who are all that and fries
All the arrogant youths I could manage
Would violently pay with their lives

Every TV chef ever recorded,
Except Rick Stein, cuz he's not a whore
Would drown in a hail of bullets
With repeats, Thursday nights, Channel 4

Then all breakfast TV presenters
Like Eamonn, Bill, Holly and Kate
Would be found dead and stiff on their sofas
As I vented my deep-seated hate.

Then the readers, if that's what you call them
Of 'Hello' and, 'Heat' and 'OK'
And all the 'celebrities' in them
Would die in a horrible way

And the charity muggers who stalk me
Demanding my time and my dosh
Would end up relieving world hunger
Once I'd rendered them down into nosh.

Next, UKIP would wholly expire
As my nuclear strikes intervened
And, frankly, quite large parts of London,
Except Hackney, on which I'm quite keen.

It's apparent that I'm mega-dangerous
I'd advise you to not get me vexed
Cuz it's easy to add an addendum
Reminding me you lot are next.

ANNA KAHN

Short Love Poem

I love you weirdly and awkwardly and fiercely.
You make no sense to me
except in my core,
where you are the only sense there is.

I am afraid
and unafraid.

There are days when you are the only thing
which can unpin the soles of my shoes from the floor
and allow me to take steps with them.
There are days when I can't move
for thinking about you.

I fear. And you -
you make me fearless.

WENDY KLEIN

Red Toenails In April

A woman who's painting her toenails red in April
is not resigned to the moment; she's thinking ahead
to summer, adventure, escape from tiresome routines.
Otherwise why keep dabbing with the wayward brush,
the unruly varnish, her hand less steady than before?
You guess it might be desperation because time
is running out, and the bottle is nearly empty.

A woman who's painting her toenails red in April
has not given up; she intends to keep her options
open; to soldier on through the rigours of ageing.
Otherwise why would she, knowing no one is likely
to notice her efforts, sit perched on the toilet seat,
her feet propped on the bidet, wielding that wayward
brush while periwinkles bloom in the woods?

A woman who's painting her toenails red in April dreads
the threat of the magnifying mirror no longer steamed up
when she's towelled dry after her long soak. Otherwise
why would she dream of absconding, of buying a ticket
to Yakutsk or Sumatra? That woman could be digging
her way out of snowdrifts, while her feet stay warm
elsewhere -- running wild to the end.

The Million Women Minus One

I've lost their latest questionnaire, along
with its covering letter, thanking me for my
previous entries which have informed
their research so they could inform me of all
the risks I have taken, based on my consumption
of alcohol, twenty years of smoking

and the size of my waistline. I remember
filling it in; sealing the freepost envelope –
would anyone return it if it wasn't free?
I remember seeing it on the front seat
of the car – a reproachful shade of white,
waiting to be posted, its subsequent

disappearance, a mystery. That they will miss
my data is certain; how else will they know
that a woman of my age can still be sexually
active; though her liver may be ballooning
in secret, or becoming sclerotic, and her brain
about to atrophy on more than the recommended

units per day? I want to throw a party and invite
all the other million women who simply break
every rule and rejoice; who lose the damn
questionnaire down the backs of their sofas;
who bin it without even bothering to fill it out,
who leave it behind in their lovers' cars.

Himself

My landlord in Llandudno had a deaf Jack Russell
that yapped and whined continuously,
snuffled at scraps that fell from the table
its square black snout twitching,
while its agile tongue hoovered up.

Sated, it would present its taut belly
for stroking, fart luxuriously,
fall asleep and snore.

Undifferentiated id, said my landlord,
and I had a vision of the man himself
in all his simplicity, clamouring
for attention, while silently
ferreting out, wolfing down,
furtive snacks, the dregs of drinks,
crawling into bed at all the wrong times
hungry, hungry, hungry.

ANDY B J LOW

Birth Of A Poet

There's a fight! There's a fight! Quick, come with me.
Gather 'round, block the view, so the teachers can't see.

There's a big gang of poets want to know who's the best
calling all-comers for a poetry contest.

Now, I'm curious and wary: "a poetry contest"?
That's an English exam? Those I detest.
Nine failed O-levels and one CSE.
Failed that as well, consistent is me.

I'd better revise and do some research.

I've read a few issues of some poetry mags,
got a feel for the stuff that's writ by these hacks.
The first thing I notice, and the next and the next,
is: it's bollocks, nothing rhymes and it's dreary as heck.

The stuff that I write is nothing like this.
I try to be open, but really, it's shit.
Obscure's the new clever, it's obtuse and "unverse",
Some new form of art with its head up its arse.

Line after line, while it's clearly not prose,
it's a catalogue of counterfeit Emperor's new clothes.

Then my musings are halted by a cacophonous roar
and I realise just how far is the stage from the door.

The bully calls out "We've not seen you before"
Makes a grab for my balls, but falls face first to the floor.
(It's a neat little trick that I've practised before.)

Thrust from the throng further into the ring,
My pen dripping blood and ready to sting.
In the silence that follows I know I will win.
I look straight in his eye.

I begin.

Secret Pool

This secret pool
Hid by an army of trees
Should be perfectly still
Not a breath, not a breeze
Yet on its smooth and shiny face
ripples form, surge forth and race
To cross, collide and intersect
The heartbeats of lovers nearly met
Patterns ignited by shards of light
Hurled through the leaves with overwhelming might
Of the blinding sun in its dying hour
The lovers must meet or the night will devour
The cooling air, the moons icy light
Will becalm the hearts and all that might
shall be lost forever in the darkness of night.

The Temptation Of Hermes

How blessed am I, that first finger of a ray of light
that slipped into your curtained room and did alight;
To brush through your hair and touch your sleeping face
and lightly kiss to steal your image;
So lovely and sublime - to hold your smile, then turn and race
away, through all the darkest depths of space.
To share you with the gods and command the planets: "Sing."
To tell the universe how could exist such beauty in a mortal being.
To beg them: grant this, my only wish, that with tomorrow's dawn
I shall return to you as flesh, as man of woman born.
To taste again that first and far too brief a kiss.
To win your heart, to one day die of bliss.

HOLLY LUHNING

From Medical Observations and Inquiries. By a Society of Physicians in London. Printed for T. Cadell and E. Johnston, in the Strand. 1776.

Case XXII. An Account of an extraordinarily sleepy Woman. By Dr Terence Brady, Physician to his Royal Highness Prince Charles of Lorrain.

I was introduced to her room
                                        five o'clock.

Her arm, stiff and heavy; a good deal of difficulty
                        to bend it-
                                                        it fell
like a piece of heavy wood. I put my mouth

to her ear; called as loud as I could.
                        She did not wake.

To be sure there was no cheat in the matter
I thrust a pin through her skin and flesh
to the bone. I kept the flame
                        of burning paper
to her cheek until I burned the skin.

I put volatile salts in her nose. Lastly
I thrust linen dipped in spirits
in her nostril   and kindled it.

All was done without the least signs of feeling.

ALWYN MARRIAGE

Lycra

I hear the hiss of tyre on tarmac
approaching fast before he comes in view,
detect a change of frequency, whiz
turning surreptitiously to hum,
as suddenly, before I know it, the close-fitting
blue and yellow backside has flashed past.

Lithe, lean and lycra-clad
he clings to handlebars and climbs
over high mountain passes,
lungs expanding with the strain,
then saved by the exhilaration of free fall
as he descends again.

Held by traction I submit
to the attraction of that muscular behind.
Tight, taut and masculine in flight,
his receding figure smooth and streamlined,
catching in the light
the rippling of a single muscle
stretched right from toe to head.

Fifty Shades Of Green

In the early years of new discovery,
childhood played and painted with
a limited palette in which sea and sky
were blue and trees were green.
Yet now, among the range of colours seen,
I can detect some fifty shades of green.

Sea green is not the same as green
of sea, and *eau-de-nile's* a shade
quite unlike the green of other rivers,
that at their birth seep from a *sludgy swamp*
then sparkle over pebbles as they
burble through the shallows.
Many miles later, growing fat with story,
rivers mature into a deep *dark green*
before they meet and mingle with the sea.

Sweeping across the Arctic skies
Aurora Borealis flirts with multicoloured hues
but prefers to decorate the dome of heaven
with all the thrill of a *fluorescent green*.

Down at sea level, in plummeting temperatures,
pack, drift and ice floe glint in northern light;
but where the chill has failed to penetrate the land,
glacier melt turns from white to purest green,
warning in its gentle way
of global catastrophe.

Green is nature's colour, home
to many more than fifty shades:
pea green, summer barley, spring wheat, grass,

Mediterranean *olive* or *almost ripening corn*.
Variegated trees take up the theme
of infinitely graded shades
in *whitebeam, willow, pine* and *birch,*
fuzzy fir and *sprightly spruce,*
robinia, and *acer, tired chestnut*
and the tasty freshness
of *young oak leaves*.

Savour on the tongue
greengage, apple, lime, cool celery,
green Chartreuse and *crème de menthe*.
Soft as *sage* or *moss* or bright as *stained glass*
in the lights of great cathedral windows,
reflecting, in the faith they celebrate,
the beauty of precious *jade* and *emerald*,
and the down to earth in *bottle green*.

Out on England's open highways,
the *A road signs* are a particular
shade that's miles away from *racing green*
or even the silk-shot shades of *petrol*.

If this list has given the impression
that green is always to be found
in beauty and delight, consider
bile and *vomit, mould* and *gangrene*,
all of which appear in delicate shades of green;
and cast your mind back to the last time
you were *sea sick*, when you almost certainly
were green around the gills.

Green can stand for ignorance or inexperience
and the poison of anyone who's *green with envy*;
but *green fingers* make our gardens grow, and *green shoots*
bring promise of recovery to an economy.

There's much to sing about, from the romantic *Greensleeves*
to the rousing, even raucous, *Green grow the rushes'O*.

The force that through the green fuse drives
the flower and Dylan Thomas's green age
is one with Hildegard's *veriditas* and our Green Man,
as well as the modern *Green Party's* concern for the environment
and the passion and commitment of a love that's *evergreen.*

Reflecting on this range
of fifty colours, it sometimes seems
that with each passing year I add
another shade of green.

Shooting The Greys

Bristling with privilege and whiskers,
he was leaning conversationally on his 12 bore

and sporting, despite warm autumn
weather, tweed jacket, collar and tie.

Pests he spat, indicating a sickly
ring-barked chestnut tree;

while high above, a drey swayed cheekily
hiding and protecting a future generation.

He looked kindly, smiles twinkled in
his eyes; on his tie the motif of a red

squirrel; on his hands blood
from shooting the greys

CLAIRE BOOKER

Stone-Whisperers

It's a neat operation,
earning front page in the Gazette –
Gang Steals Valuable Pavements.
Whole streets have walked, folded
in fleece, packed on pallets then trucked away.
A century of footfall skimmed: imprints
of hobnail, flappers' heels, fag-end burns,
hop-scotch, trikes, drunks, the herringbone
of lovers' feet all untimely ripped
along with flag and sett.

This stone's been filched before –
delver crouched in quarry pit, listened
for a quickening of natural fault, rived out
hidden form, older than the first push
of Alpine peaks. Now it's winched again,
on the swindle, whilst we kerb-skip to detour,
barely note the grunt and guts of it. Hard gold
cretaceous: withstands time and weather
but not these stone rustlers' jemmies.
They'll be down your way tomorrow, stealing
history from under your feet.

Is This What A Mother's Bones Become?

Stoked on hard dreaming, I climb the stairwell –
stop at the extra turn at the top, the swell

of the door jamb, toothed with its steel trim.
Bees-wax wrestles damp. Damp wins.

Inside I find her gaunt: hair magnesium streaks
stuck to her head, though her rouged cheeks

still ride those bones high. Below, she's barely
dressed; legs clamped like a child who badly

needs to let go of the body's tyranny.
Truth is, there's been a slow rubbing away

since we last met. The brass, once clearly etched,
no longer brings her fresh to me at night.

This latest copy, a Chinese whisper, leans
into the kitchen, talks intimately to a man.

I see only his vast, uninvited bulk fling
shadow across the room. There's nothing

left to say. She lifts a chopping board, tired –
as work must tire when you're five years dead.

This is not my mother. Or has she now assumed,
in some slant way, aspects of the room?

Clatter of expert dicing: beetroot, apple, dill
all fall to her blade. No matter – she feeds me still.

Unpeeled

Freud's having a field day, sharpening
his pencil in that 'train through tunnel' kind of way,
chewing me over with his second best organ.
He scrawls *onion* across my ribs.
But who needs tears on a night like this?
I'm all cock a doodle, riding a Bratwurst so ample
it straddles the plate. This lady's a boy-girl, reeling
in the breadth of it: twitching dowsing stick
and rawl-plug all rolled into one. Hips jut, flip it
just like a fella walking the beast, tight on its leash.
Curious hound, ears pricked, snouting
for the roar of underground rivers.

THOMAS THURMAN

On First Looking Into An A To Z

My talent (or my curse) is getting lost:
my routes recondite and esoteric.
Perverted turns on every road I crossed
have dogged my feet from Dover up to Berwick.
My move to London only served to show
what fearful feast of foolishness is mine:
I lost my way from Tower Hill to Bow,
and rode the wrong way round the Circle Line.
    In nameless London lanes I wandered then
    whose tales belied my tattered A to Z,
    and even now, in memory again
    I plod despairing, Barking in my head,
still losing track of who and where I am,
silent, upon a street in Dagenham.

Not April In Paris

The sea lies solid under ice;
The blizzard seldom stops;
The *glogi*'s running freely
In friendly coffee shops;
The trams still run and life goes on
And still I can't remember
Why no-one ever calls a song
"Helsinki in November".

Do Not Kowtow

When I am old, as owned by wrinkled skin,
and not by thought, since I'm already old,
do not kowtow to what you see. Within
the wrinkled skin's a child of three years old,
a teenager in terror of his sin,
a twenty-two year old in love, an old
and bitter fool, whose inspiration's thin;
when I am full of tales, and sick, and old,
do not kowtow to old and wrinkled skin.

Too Many Sonnets

"Too many sonnets", growls the curt rejection.
Too many sonnets? Can the news be true?
This polished work is workshopped to perfection,
a classic form reworked to something new.
But still, I'll keep them coming while I'm living,
and when I'm old and sinking into death
I'll write a final sonnet of thanksgiving
and gasp the sestet in my final breath.
    And then, in death, what nightmares may inspire?
    Within the circle of the realms infernal
    reserved for sonneteers, I'll write in fire
    to send to *Styx Review*, or some such journal,
and if there's surplus sonnets there in hell ...
well... then I may compose a villanelle.

TRACEY MARION

Anorexia Nervosa

When I first started dropping the weight,
Everyone was like WOW, you look great,
Tell me your secret so I can be like you!
Tell me how I can be thin and miserable too.

Strangers gaped at my thighs,
And though I knew it was unwise,
I let no morsel pass my lips
I feared would end up on my hips.

Strangers gaped at my thighs,
And my thighs gaped too –
The fat and muscle shrinking
To let the daylight through.

Once I'd shed every lump
and bump
I also lost my hair in clumps,
And feeling frozen to my core,
I shivered every day and wore:
Thermal leggings, thermal socks, thermal vest,
Two coats to go over the rest,
Thermal jumper, thermal hat,
What would Gok Wan think of that?

So sure I was onto a winner,
My boyfriend couldn't help with dinner,
Everything he heated up made me melt down,
And even out and about in town,
I couldn't find a thing to eat,
A meal was torture, not a treat.

I was a disappearing act!
Vanishing right in front of you,
Picking at and pushing food away,
And still my partner chose to stay.

When things hit rock bottom,
He rode with me in the ambulance,
The height of modern romance.

He read Battle Royale to me
In A&E
To the alarm of the nurse;
It was a great reminder
Things could always be worse.

Then I started eating again – it was a revelation,
Taste itself was education,
I discovered once more the pleasure of meals,
When you've starved for months, everything appeals:

Doughnuts, chocolate, cake and sweets,
Toast, roasts, fish and meat,
Twiglets, omelette, fruity jelly
I wanted all of it to get in my belly.

I had a few… queasy days,
When I might have overdone it a little,
But my periods had stopped
And my bones were still brittle,

I could argue that hot chocolate
With cream and marshmallows
Was practically medicine
And needed to be swallowed.

Gradually I gained the weight back
And with it the ability to be myself,
To connect with other people again,
And a second chance at health.

So why am I airing my dirty laundry?
Cause it could happen to you or your brother or auntie,
Though food and weight's all I've talked about now,
Controlling your life with your diet somehow?
It doesn't work, it makes things worse, it's self-harm in disguise
Plus every shape is fucking great and so is every size.

Tracey Marion won the first Guildford Keystone Pub Slam with her performance of this poem on July 9th 2014.

NANCY CHARLEY

Classification: *Ursus Consolativus*

I'm fussing through archives splitting hairs
over information and record, evidence or representation
whose content, context, structure are authentic.

A den of stashed racks, box upon acid-free box,
all uncatalogued. I must read each document
to locate the one quotation needed for a thesis.

No escape. No *Open Sesame.*
Then your text:
The lovely bones of a living bear.

From mussy hibernation, fur's reek.
I finger seed, tangle, tick. Find skin.
Clamber through tissue and vessel to wrap arms

around defined muscle, toes wriggle down femurs.
I nestle against vertebrae, settle in a rib cocoon,
offer honey, pillow your heart.

AMY MCALLISTER

At Risk

He was forever stuffing junior infants in the bottom of the can machine.
Like as if their sweetness meant they should be stored amongst the cokes.
They seldom cried.
Partly out of shock, partly out of glimpsing fizzy drinks they
Regularly lifted from the fridge in Jim's into the trolley
Only to be scolded at the checkouts.
He liked how cleanly some would fit
And often removed their Velcroed shoes,
arranging them in natural-looking footstep formations
Leading to the base of the machine.
And once a child was neatly tucked away,
He would go back to class and be a better pupil,
Sharing out the crayons and remembering to use the red for hearts
And not for shading head wounds.

Wintery Thoughts

Tonight, as I cram my hot water bottle
Back into its pastel lavender fleece
After its annual wash,
It occurs to me that I will one day
Be cramming the arms of some unfortunate baby
Into a fleece of a similar colour.

I really hope I don't get cold feet.

Microcosm

Locked out again,
Not knowing when
A spare key would scrape me safe,
At dusk, Julie's mammy coaxed me in,
Concealing that she thought it such a sin
For me to be be-stoopèd like a scrawny waif.

My first microwave experience then.
Corn popping as quickly as the pockets of my childhood bubble wrap.
Each kernel bursting under the pressure,
A searing blossom born of heat and hate,
Salty, sharp and raring to create,
Then left to stand for one electric minute.

And I had stood for many more, this day and many days before,
Wanting to be melted down like butter to be swirled into the wood of my front door.
To hide,
Or for my family's pride,
Or to be widely reported as to have mysteriously died.
Not on a rotating plate,
For people who don't like to wait,
And don't much mind if what comes out doesn't taste great.
I listened for the popping to slow down,
And knew when I was older I'd leave town.

And in their kitchen-dining room extension
I saw an unfamiliar lack of tension.
No pop culture here. Only popcorn.

PATRICK B OSADA

On The Red Light

The consummate professional :
Chatting, to put me at my ease.
Gently he helps me to prepare :
Attentive - then deftly prompting,
Questioning - polishing my speech.

And I feel fine : with thoughts marshalled,
My favourite phrases practised , checked,
I'm eloquent and in control.

"I think we're ready now," he says,
"*We're rolling when the red light shows.*"

And on the red light thoughts escape,
Eloquence evaporates as
I become a stuttering wreck -
Tongue almost tied….

Always on the
Red light it's the same : confidence
Withers, lines are fluffed, the simplest
Truth stays lodged in my dry throat.
Always at these times I need my best -
Instead, thick tongued, I croak, whisper
All of life's most important lines
Like….*"I love you, love you, love you."*

Presence

(At Barbara Hepworth's Trewyn Studios and Museum, St. Ives.)

They should place a sign here reading
"*Back in five minutes*." Here as left,
your work smocks hang behind the door,
tools still lie where they were dropped - work
has only briefly stopped. It may
be luck - or artifice, perhaps -
but it's as if you've slipped away.
"*Gone out for lunch*" or "*Popped next door*"
are messages we might expect
left propped against your last maquette.

Gone thirty years and more… it's true,
yet all seems well and life means all
it ever meant. Out of sight can
never mean you're out of mind. Your
garden flourishes as planned, where
mute sculptures stand as monuments
to talent and to taste. And could
it be the same for everyone -
to slip away as you have done?
to tantalise and seemingly
to wait so close : ephemeral
as scent on air; in the next room
perhaps, somewhere about the house?

Wild Ransoms

Along the cliff edge -
Too far to safely reach -
These white bells tantalised
With their strange scent :
A pungent odour on the breeze
Their signature.

Later, in Roseland,
We saw them grown like weeds :
Filling meadows, smothering hedgerow grass,
Covering the roadside verge
Like gentle drifts of snow.

And at St. Just, filling the churchyard there,
Bluebells and ransoms like a haze
On every bank, round ancient graves.

And, through the palm
That grows where you now rest,
A solitary ransom flower had set.

Though far away in miles and time,
The smell of garlic takes me back -
Transports me instantaneously
To that Spring day :
The tiny church, the muddy creek,
The ransom flowers and you.

MARY PARGETER

Ashes To Ashes

Tipped into a cube of earth,
in a cloud of white dust.
Tumbling mix, body and bone, mingling ash,
ash of teeth, ash of ankle,
ash of passion, ash of anguish.
Bone white ashes, damaged ashes,
sent away from home ashes,
three children and barely twenty ashes,
money's tight ashes, ash of athlete,
business ashes, five star ashes,
ash of operations,
too early, too late ashes.
Ashes that lie alone. Goodbye ashes.
Ashes of genes, feet from your ash
half circle the square
brown shoes, shiny shoes,
fashion shoes, pointed shoes,
high heel shoes.
In the small brown square
white ash luminiscent in its clay cube
and a final dark covering.

goodbye rob

Goodbye Rob,
You handsome devil
You wisecracker
You charmer.

Cheers Rob,
You Burgundy, Barolo, Bollinger,
Chardonnay, Chablis, Courvoisier,
Dubonnet, Drambuie, draught,
Sandemans Sherry. Shaker,
Stirrer, pourer and drinker.
'Top-up anyone?'

Bye Rob,
You natty dresser
You Prince of Wales,
Three piece check
Suited smarmer.
You pencil-thin tash
30s smoothie.

So long Rob,
The ladies loved you
Turn on the charm
With a witty line.

'Hello blue eyes'
Well, hello.
You romantic
You misogynist
You lover of women.

Cheerio Rob,
You melancholy depressive

You despondent
You politician basher
You cynic
You chooser of drinks
You filler of glasses
And dreamer to love songs.

Farewell Rob,
To the laughs, the drinks,
The boozers, the eccentrics,
The late night sleepovers
The early morning hangovers,
For tea at Kennards
And 'G&T, darling'
On your lips.

GEOFFERY PIMLOTT

Window

my window saw
a man beat a dog,beside some car
with no wheels,
jacked up on bricks,
from the night before;
and a dusty black, once blue,
coal truck, stationary rumbling;
heaving shouldered sacks
down the alley;
whilst the horse-drawn milk float
chomps grass,
as bottles clink on doorsteps
up and down our street.

In The Eastern Highlands Of Papua New Guinea

i bought a tin of corned beef
in a dust bowl store
in a dust bowl town
in red earth mountains
quite near The Pacific Rim
the meat inside was dirt brown:
the dust bowl butcher was no better
let red blood drip out of green-slime meat
trying to decide if it was fit to eat:
in the market at the back of town
women sold mildewed peanuts

laid out on the ground
then earthquake shaken
seven on the Richter Scale
everywhere swaying
amidst the massive roar
the weevils ate the lentils
bought in the dust bowl store:
the earth runs red when it rains at two
and mountains seep volcanic smoke
as i walk tracks in wantok time
quite near The Pacific Rim

Harps Oak Lane

let me tell you
what we saw
in Harps Oak Lane
before we enter
Markedge
in the mist and rain

cow parsley campian
bluebell stitchwort
bedeck the way
through Harps Oak's
Spring mist April day
dark trees' spiked twigs
claw back that shroud
that tracks each
potholed twist and bend
past unseen woods
and fields hedge lined
to Harps Oak end
at Markedge
in the mist and rain

LORRI PIMLOTT

Bloomsbury Afternoon

In the Egyptian room
At the British Museum,
Painted faces on caskets
Reflect my gaze impassively.
Inside, the sere husks,
That once breathed and moved
And laughed and wept and loved
Now sleep alone for ever,
Untouched and untouching.

Outside, a busker
plays Plaisir d'amour
Upon a silver flute
The sweet notes rise
Above the city noise,
Then scatter on ground
Like the petals of the roses
You once gave me.

Raymond

This book I love,
Sweet Raymond stole it
For me, gave it with
Such gentle pleasure
In bringing me a gift
I found no words to
Name the wrong of it.

And now, its browned
And brittle pages
Breath out passed time
And soft-eyed Ray
Hangs out in no where
Upon a silky thread
Of sad remembrance.

Survarnabhumi Airport, Bangkok

Another day, another journey.
Outside the window as we rise,
Bangkok wakes, and coughing,
Tugs at the soiled hem of daybreak.
This is the City of the Angels.
Above it, mighty wings cleave the air.

'I was a teacher,' said Miss Noi.
My father is old. I care for him.
We came here for the peace,
For birdsong in the morning,
The scent of jasmine in the evening.
My father is old, he does not understand
Where the quiet has gone. He is afraid.

High above her, held in a metal womb,
We soar into the clouds above the city.
Below, the old man weeps and trembles.

BETHANY W POPE

Sacred Animals

All infants need redemption, even this
male must be presented at the temple.
His parents purchased two downy-breasted
pigeons outside the gates from a snag-toothed
man who smiled at their fortune - their first child
would be circumcised, would need no dowry.
He had sold out of doves, but these birds were
unblemished, acceptable according
to law. The family was split crossing the
threshold. The mother went to huddle with
the women behind a screen. The father
bore his adopted son in one hand, bound
birds in the other - they flapped a bit, but
were used to the bizarre actions of men.
The priest wrung two sets of small vertebra
above the altar, appropriate prayers
echoed on stone. There was not much spilled blood.
Of course, there was a hymn sung. Life was bought
with two small sparks, some flesh, a few tender
bones. Nothing was wasted; when the service
was finished, the priest had a meal. The child,
blessed, would flourish and grow beyond this death.
At that time, each life had a set price, birds
for babies, lambs for men. Far outside the
temple gates Golgotha waited. Even
then the soil was formed from skull-dust and skin.
There were not enough animals on earth
to save all of us. Redemption required
a different sacrifice: new flesh, strange blood.

In Borrowed Robes

The man is easily in his eighties,
shrunken in an old tweed suit, a plastic
yellow daffodil pinned to his lapel.
He stands before a room of poets, speaks
at great length of his love for a man who
died at half his age. Still trying to shrug
into the long-dried skin of Thomas, he
recites verses 'in the style of", acts out
the opening of 'Under The Milkwood'.
I see what he would have liked to become,
had he the courage to create
without imitating. As it is, he's
bound himself to the shadow of an old
idea. His life's become a borrowed robe.

CAT RANDLE

A Stranger in my own Century

***A Found Poem:* Each of these lines comes from interaction on the Internet (apart from IRL which used to mean In Real Life)**

White noise is incorrectly assumed to come from white light

IRL It's a difference in generations, not all of my life is my own

What's on your mind?

IRL My children think all information is shared

Not often will you hear me say go Google

White light has no hue, it contains all the wavelengths of the visible spectrum

I give in u can't sit and write a chapter when your husband has decided to tidy up the house

White noise resembles a /sh/ sound in "ash"

Where is the Cheeseburger?

We are working on poetry exercises so read with care

In Asia Black is associated with the disorder that brings life

If you are in Wellington (NZ) are you okay?

IRL I would not go into a market place and give away pictures of my children to strangers.

Okay I am officially peopled out. I will resurface on Wednesday evening

Black is the colour of experience

IRL The person you are on Facebook is not the person you are in real life

White noise resembles a /sh/ sound in "ash"

Throwing out threads waiting

White noise is incorrectly assumed to come from white light

Heartbreak

Rosemary hung on
The midnight air
Between sheeted lashes
Half closed eyes
Yield more passion
Than this kiss of herb

From this promethean heat
There is no release

To hear your heart breathe
And your breath beat
As I lie
On the edge
Perched ready to fly

But there is no wind
And the heat sinks into my lungs
As roots into a soil

If I fly
To know I can never return
Is crueller than this kiss of herb

STEPHEN ROSS

Perspectives

What's a perspective? Your single view,
With mine too, or do you slew my true?
Take Ireland's tricolour, it's representative,
Three's so few. Already knew didn't you?

Green is seen as free Republic. It means,
For others envy 'n' jealousy, slicks of sick!
For me it's natures love. Heals better than
A health systems shoves in gloves, Pathetic!

Next white, so bright, see peace do you
Between the two, or cowardly surrender?
So subjective this reflective directive. Ego
For me I see, ergo male and female power.

Last is orange, hold! 'tis gold, so I'm told.
I see double! Ulster's trouble now rubble!
Traffic lights, ready to alightite or mend bends,
Yet for me it's divinities creative certainty.

Perspectives right, have might, often fight.
For their right to ignite the brightest light!
So I now go, so very slow, so I may know.
Please just accept, I suspect, all are correct.

The Dream (What does it mean?)

I woke up this morning, with a dream in my head
A row of straight houses, faces angled with dread

With the exception of one, a most beautiful sight
not quite in dead centre, rather off to the right

A curved yellow cottage, with hazel windows of pine
Inside a robin red breast was gently drinking some wine

I'd been down this road, several times here before
So why had I never seen it, so colourful and unexplored.

The name on the doorstep said welcome, please no boots
I began to get excited, my heart raced like chaotic flutes

I pressed upon the knocker, it gave way unexpectedly
Soft, smooth and silky, not taut and stiff like me

Instead of a door knob, this door was quite weird
threads of delicate cotton bristled up as I neared

The cotton door prised open as I caressed its pink lock
A crack gave way gently. Screams! Yes, I should certainly have knocked

A light oozed from the hallway, windows shattered from sounds
As I crept gingerly forward, terrified by what I might find.

As I peeked round the corner, a most interesting sight
The red breasted robin was having a fight

I watched with amusement and particular glee
As the bird manoeuvred skilfully upon a blue tree

The branches swung wildly wrapping round robin's trunk
As the leaves scattered gracefully leaving puddles of junk

The two combatants, done fighting, collapsed in a heap
Wrapped round one another, no longer able to leap

Having enjoyed the drama and understanding it dead
I crept from the house and woke up in my bed.

CHRYS SALT

Hymn To Mastectomy

Here's to the woman with one tit
who strips down to her puckered scars
and fronts the mirror – doesn't give a shit
for the pert double-breasted wonderbras
sneaking a furtive gander
at her missing bit.

'Poor lady,' they are thinking,
'can her husband bear to touch her?
Will she ever dare to wear
that slinky low-cut sweater?'

Here's to the lady with half a bust
who wears her lack of symmetry
with grace and moist with lust
offers a single nipple like a berry
to her lover's tongue.
Here's to the single-breasted ones
come home, victorious from their wars
wearing the wounds
as badges on the chests
of Amazons.

'She ought to cover up,
it's embarrassing, it's shocking.
I'm sure she thinks she's very brave
but everybody's looking!'

Here's to those wondrous affrontages
out on the scene in sauna, pool and gym,
those who when whole were dying –
now less than whole
become themselves again.

Waltz Time

they're doing the Alzheimer Waltz
the one two three Alzheimer Waltz
the tune is an oldie
beyond all recall
but they pivot and twirl
on a sixpence of dreams
his suit double breasted
her stockings with seams
all sense disconnected
unplugged from the wall
they're doing the Alzheimer Waltz

waltz of forgetfulness
danced in a wilderness
caught between
somewhere and been there before
they know all the steps
but can't think what they're for
in the one two three
Alzheimer Waltz

they're doing the Alzheimer Waltz
the one two three Alzheimer Waltz
on snub slippered feet
that forget they remember
the dance tunes of spring-time
in dying December
they shimmy and swirl
light fantastic unerring
a dashing young soldier
a slip of a girl
in the one two three
Alzheimer Waltz

waltz of forgetfulness
danced in a wilderness

caught between
somewhere and been there before
they know all the steps
but can't think what they're for
in the one two three Alzheimer Waltz

they're doing The Alzheimer Waltz.
the one two three Alzheimer Waltz
and the lights on the tree
are as bright as the light
in the eyes of the dancers
who take to the floor
in the one two three
one two three
one two three
one two three
one two three Alzheimer Waltz

With Adrian At The Peace Festival

in memory of Adrian Mitchell

if you saw him running, it was because he'd spotted truth in the crowd and was going after it if you saw him smiling it was at a good deed waving from a balcony if you saw him jumping it was in a playground with all the other daft kids on the block raising anarchy if you heard him singing it was 'girls and boys come out to play' if you saw him laughing, he was laughing he was really laughing if you saw him waving it was to say come in and join the feast of the human race if you saw him writing it was a love letter to the world on the day of its crucifixion if you saw him dancing it was to a Beetles tune about giving peace a chance and waiting for that moment to arrive.

PAULINE SEWARDS

Pictures On The Radio

(found poem: February 2014)

Sky is bruised liver as I grip the steering wheel tightly breathe
down the motorway, reversing the morning's journey
Mishal Husain has turned into affable Eddie Mair who's
promising to interrupt himself when Britain goes for gold.
The skeleton has been around since at least 1927. I have no idea
what it looks like. Overtaking
in the lorry's dismal slipstream I hear
'Dunkirk without the war' 'Stoical pensioners' '80 mph
down ice.' 'She's done it!!!!' I remain with eyes on the road,
chronically peeved - with a tear for fearless champions,
the power of story, drive into the turn off queue, try to see what
the other drivers are listening to.

Patti Smith And The Rules For Life

I wrap the book up in brown paper
and I send it with a letter in the fly leaf
where she put a kiss next to the X in the middle of your name
I saw her on the South Bank
taking pictures of her picture in a window and I knew her by her skinny jeans
her Lennon specs
her woollen hat
the fine outline of her moustache
and the picture in the window
of a day in Coney Island
She was in London for the signing
in the bookshop with the rain outside
and she stood up for the photographers
with a beatific smile
and did they pixellate it when she spat upon the stage and she sent them away when the flashes hurt her eyes and she sang to us as if she were in a stadium
in the bookshop with the rain outside
she sang of Coney Island and the Chelsea Hotel
and of Blakean Angels
and she said *don't be afraid to sing along*
don't be afraid to look uncool
there's no one here uncool as me
and I didn't believe her
but I did believe in the Blakean Angels
in the awkward grandeur and intercession of angels.
.I've never rated giving advice
maybe that's why when you phoned tonight
you asked me for direction
but I hardly know the way to go myself
so we'll sing of Blakean Angels

we'll tape paper to walls and we'll draw till we get it right we'll buy our clothes from the Mind shop
and fill up our notebooks to tell back our days
talk bravely to strangers, dance barefoot in rain
take photos of windows and cranes.
I wrap the book up in brown paper
and I send it with a letter in the fly leaf
where she put a kiss next to the X in the middle of your name.

Brighton 1980

If cities were the schools in which we learned
you were a town learning to become a city.
'Ocean's bauble', bubble, shoals of lovers
dancing through the all night streets, loose haired,
and ankle chained
to the hedonistic puzzle.

SHADWELL SMITH

Philip Larkin Look-Alike

He's a drop dead ringer in a certain shade.
You could pick him out in a line up parade.
That's him! No doubt. Like a long lost brother.
Can't tell the real one from the other.
Doppelganger- lammer ding-dong.
Look at that; Mysteron man , jazz cravat.
Can't do the voice but don't take the mike.
He's a Philip Larkin look-alike.

He's opened pubs, clubs, a Russian sub
a place that sells Croatian grub.
Did a walk on, walk off ferry appearance,
An 'everything must go' carpet clearance.
He's the face that launched a thousand grips
at a Judo hustle club called 'Nips'.
Cut the ribbon at a local landfill site.
He's a Philip Larkin look-alike.

His Elastoplast smile hides the yellow teeth
of the garage mechanic that lies beneath,
the 2 for 1 specs and the trademark strop
'Parents - Don't they fuck you up'.
Give them what they want, sign a few chests,
kind regards and All the best's.
By day he fixes motorbikes
But by night-
He's a Philip Larkin look-alike.

Hat

It wasn't all that special
or particularly rare,
just a fur hat
that travelled with you
on the bus
and everywhere
you went
while you were out.

Left on the hook
with the other hats
and gloves
and coats
when you got to work.

It wasn't even proper fur
just a simulated piece
of female chic
set upon your head
but never merely functional.

It was, instead
something that you'd tilt
slightly to the right
to assume the style
of Clara Bow
just before you left
the house
and down the road
towards your stop.

Nothing much to speak of
just a silly thing
to keep you warm
and use as something
of a prop
to help you through
your day.
But I loved it
as I loved you
anyway.

Tommy

I think, if I'm right
it was a Sunday
at Her Majesty's.
Just after the Cossack dancers
and before that
long break in transmission.

In-between you lurched
meticulously
through each inept stumble
and incompetent slip.
Navigating every staged disaster
with a master's broad hand.

We loved you for that
and the way you had
of making us believe
that our own floppy feet
might somehow walk us through
unaided to the end.

And as you fell
very slowly to the floor;
people laughed
and I laughed too
until the curtain came across
and someone dragged you through.

Then there was no more.

ELAINE STABLER

The Skeleton Named Linda

For thirty-nine years she hid
in the closet of my mother's mind.
Creeping, crawling
through the depths of deep dark thoughts.
Wait,
Where's the key? Lock it away.
Not to be haunted today.

Baby baby, darling child
pretty in pink,
soft blue eyes.
She sent her away,
to hide
like a skeleton, in the depths of her
broken mind.

She was not dead,
she did not die.
In fact she lived,
she lived a different life,
with a different mother,
in a different time.

But the thought,
the memory of her remains.
The baby skeleton.
Silent, sleeping, creeping.
in my poor mother's mind.

My Fondest Painting *(for Norman)*

I wish my memories were paintings.
I could encase my fondest in glass,
Then the paper would not crease,
And the faces would not wrinkle
They would never cease
To last.

In my fondest painting of you,
There is a smile drawn upon your face,
We sit amongst the carpet coloured bar stools,
Letting the cigarette smoke burn away.

The table is framed by a Jack, the King
And a Queen's head on a 10p.
The cards, they are wrinkled
Amongst the laughter
And the eyes that could not see.

Another drink, another round
Ready Salted crisps for the little girl
My precious painting reads,
Stay for one more, Phil.

I wish you could see my painting
Through my eyes.
I wish I could tell you
How it felt,
That with you,
Some of my fondest childhood memories died.

But we shall not fret, and we shall not worry.
You are safe, encased in glass,

In my memory.
My dear Fondest,
Paintings encased in glass,
Are always the finest.

PAUL SUTHERLAND

Appeal To A House Sparrow

for Farrah

Sparrow, Sparrow - they've taken my granddaughter away from me

Quick Little Phillip - they've taken my granddaughter away

In the bare thicket of a hedgerow the rain's trickling down

You chirp away, on your own today, chirruping half the day

My Settled Spuggie – you gone quiet, and now is only rain

Trickling winkling down through the thickset of a hedgerow

Homely Cheeper – I've spent a lifetime or more to you listening

Sailor of the Eaves – if you big ears, tilt your head listen to my plea

If you A Lost Soul Catcher, you biggest wings, bring her safe to me

Bird of Far Arrival – they've taken my granddaughter away from me.

Nipissing Stillness

The afternoon pontoon ship plies; its engine purrs. A giant feline carries me to the sunny islands. Water moves in patterns of stillness, like long radio waves, in flights of slight undulations. Each low swell a far expanded wing. Sand flies envelop the Chief Commanda II, named after chiefs of the Nipissing people going back to the War of 1812. The insect swarm doesn't bite. Other boats alter the delicate fluid designs, timid uniform swells parallel at times across the open blue-greyness. Creases, shaving nicks, mark the lake's face. Tender water-skin ripples, no white caps or peaks or troughs. The ferry pushes on, through heat, crossing formations, cross-paths of invisible birds. Quietude deepens. The high sun builds tall water-pillars that shimmer and vanish into the depths. A shallow lake easily aroused, so placid. Nearing the five islands its appearance changes, dim movement annotates the tranquillity. One landfall slides past, off the port, revealing further drops of green earth in the background. Serene varied greens, white sandy beaches. A flotilla of ducks pass between the islands in the distance a black line moving across the haze. The biggest island un-touched, a broadleaved forest down to its shore, a floating plateau of the Precambria shield. In the straits the surface adornment changes to minute ribs of plaid. Sacred islands carry in turn a curse. Story of starvation after war, a native woman with special powers sent to bring help, returns to the islands to see all its dying survivors gone, not a trace, not of bodies, of belongings or of violence. A caldera of volcanoes millenniums ago gives the shaped quintet an insular symmetry. No wave-white breaks around rocky out-posts. 'Islands of the Sky' look blood-bound by a hidden desire. Unbeached lands. *Sound of silence* is playing in the lost background from the cruising boat's horned loud speakers. Taunt lines, wrinkles, aging marks, sound marks: the half-waves resemble the moving backs of abundant shiny fish. Lines criss-cross; the lake's pointed with subtle chain mail, each subdued rise and fall joined. Minor crinkles over the deeper oscillations, each flowing miniature blemish like a scratch. The engine kneads, and claws, the boat turns from The Mantious back towards its home harbour's speech. Unhindered light creates the mirage of glowing curtains, like a reversed Northern Lights, rising from rolling passivity. Cirrus reflected in an unified stream; the wake's intricate white beading trims the constant dark-blue-grey. Suddenly calm water of Nipissing is intimate with my dreams.

Last Of May First Of June

Crêpe de Chine-iris
has no scent, but if I could
ask the moths, then what?

For the illumined east
our green-berry holly makes
a stain-glass window

A purple foxglove's
deep finger-hole quivers from
an entering bee

A delta-winged bug
touches down on our small lawn -
red and grey ensigns

Late evening awakes
with one pinkish star above
blue and red closed cups.

KATHY TYTLER

Walking Home At Midnight: Monday

We leave thick mist on Kennetside
Climbing the steps to Kings Road;
the air clears,
Lit up in flashing blue by speeding cars.

We walk through town,
Shop-fitters are working in Ann Summers.
Large men with smiling faces,
and the man with the guitar sings in his usual place.

A half moon hangs low over Oxford Road,
a segment of ripe blood orange.
A woman embraces her man in a passionate Goodbye,
then curses loudly
as she drops her can.
Special Brew foams into the gutter ...
But we are looking at the stars.

Walking Home At Midnight: Thursday

She stopped me to ask the way,
Just before midnight, last Thursday
She spoke of bars I did not know,
But I recognised one, name of Lola Lo.

"Escape to the tropical bounty island,
And party, live life to the full."
Escape to where the bright young things
Get drunk and maybe even pull.

Away from town. She had been heading
Towards the grittier streets of West Reading
Away from the night-life and the bright lights
She was young, dressed to party on this cold night.

Her heels were high, her shoulders bare
Turn around, I said, go back to where
There's clubs and bars and neon lights
And bouncers to stop alcohol fuelled fights.

You're going in the wrong direction, love,
Go back the way you came,
Don't stray onto Oxford Road dressed like that,
They'll think you're on the game.

Turn round and take first left, first right
Go back to Lola Lo
A place I frequented when I was young
Many years ago

In those days called The Tudor Tavern
Where Eric the folksinger sang,
Each Sunday night; The Wild Rover
And we would sing along ...

> *And it's no, nay, never,*
> *No nay never no more*
> *Will I play the wild rover*
> *No never no more*

Yes, we knew how to enjoy ourselves then
Even though the last bus left at half ten
When half a lager could be bought for ten pence
And we wore coats in winter – we had sense!

So turn around now my love
Go back to Lola Lo
Go back to those streets of fun
That I left long ago ...

GARETH TOMS

Trying To Figure It Out

When all has gone wrong
when confusion is ruling
and an answer just can't be found,
don't try to pin down lost love with guessed logic
the pair won't cross in each other's bounds.

When two are subtracted
to make one and one
the result is a negative equation,
and the two may never be
added together again
despite one unit's persuasion.

It's this division that multiplies
a certain sadness in the sum,
which is now cancelled-down
to a single figure:
but everything starts with one.

And somewhere there's another one
with hopes for a positive equation,
and then all will seem quite logical
with addition on a future occasion.

My Favourite Liquid

Alcohol used to be
my favourite liquid
hand to mouth
it would help me to express

but now I favour
a liquid that does not
lead me to indulge
to embarrassing excess.

My now favourite liquid is
a more graceful communicator
it playfully records my
ideas as I think

it helps me to remember
instead of wanting to forget
I celebrate, not commiserate
with ink.

THOMAS VLIESTRA

Sugar Daddy

My name's Mr. Stiles, can I get you something?
A coffee, a tea, a blueberry muffin?
No
Okay. I represent SugarDaddy.com.
But you already know that or you wouldn't have come along.
Now, thanks to politicians of the current Coalition
You have problems funding your degree: your fees and tuition.
At Sugar Daddy we don't like to see destroyed ambitions
So why don't I outline our terms and conditions,
To make it clear what you are getting yourself in for.
And if you have any concerns, I'm here to reassure.

We offer flexible hours and a chance to meet diverse people.
Have fun while you work, which we assure you is legal.
Now this job isn't for the weak or the feeble,
But looking at you, you seem as bold as the eagle
Sharp as a tack, pretty as a pearl;
Let's get to business and talk about making you a rich girl.

Will it undermine my self-worth?
Destroy my self-esteem? Will I
Come home feeling dirty? Will this
Shatter all my dreams?

(But with the fees increasing
And with job prospects decreasing
I don't know ...
Do I really have a choice?)

I have a couple of questions, if that's okay?

How long do I sign on for? How much do I get paid?
How long does your course last?
                                        About three years.
Oh, that will fly past! Have no fear.
                                                Well...
                                                        I was just wondering...
As for pay, we say about six hundred a month.
It's like a maintenance loan with extra money for fun.
You'd be contracted until the end of your degree -
Leave any earlier and we won't pay your fees.

So how often do I have to meet clients?

Well that's up to them, on them you're reliant.
Our company doesn't look fondly on non-compliance,
Do you **want** to end up a Bachelor of Science?
Or not?
        I do.
                Great. Did you bring your application?
                                                Yes.
                                                        This all looks fantastic.
Shall we start negotiation?
                                Sure.
And just to reiterate
you're signed on till graduation
                                        I know.
Well, first thing we require is
a short demonstration.
                            Will it undermine my self-worth?
                            Destroy my self-esteem? Will I
                            Come home feeling dirty? Will this
                            Shatter all my dreams?

                            But with the fees increasing
                            And with job prospects decreasing
                            I don't know...

Do I really have a choice?

A demonstration?

Yes, about what you ticked on your list
To see if you were telling the truth, or taking the piss.

Huh?

Well - the more you're willing to do
the more money you'll make.
Let's go through it here to see if you made a mistake.
Oral Sex? Tick.
Anal Sex? No.
Dress up? What does this say?
Orgies? No.
Shame really - that can make you extra tips.

We're in public! Stop this!

It says here you're willing to kiss.
That's nice really, as a lot of girls won't offer that.

Stop.

Well, there was one girl from Hull, but she was well…a bit fat.

Are you listening to me?
ARE YOU LISTENING TO ME?!
Sorry, I didn't mean to shout.

I'm trying to help you out.

OK – well - you're embarrassing me.

Fine, there's the door.

Look - I want to do it, but
don't treat me like a whore.

But clients will do that. I'm sorry I did.

I guess I need to get used to it.

Well ...You have to commit…

Anyway ... what's this about a demonstration?

Well - you need to come back to my place, or your accommodation.
And we'll go through your list and see what you can do.
Then you can sign on the dotted line and
I'll put a price on you.

SUE KUCKO

Once I Had A Secret Love

Once I had a secret love
that nestled in between my legs
I had to shout for him to stop
in case he fertilized my eggs...
Now I shout it from the highest hill -
My new doctors' put me on the pill
And I screw round like a whore
Because I can't get pregnant anymore.

So I told my best friend Debs
in a drunken reverie
She said 'Sex has gone to your head
And you may have an STD'
Well I went to the clinic today
Legs asunder, my bits on display
And I will have to abstain
At least until next Friday anyway……

As a young girl I was always making up new (and generally saucy) words for old songs. My mother used to chastise me for having 'the sense of humour of an aging barmaid'. I have to admit she was probably right. So here it is...the little ditty that I made up at the tender age of fifteen whilst waiting for my best friend's new boyfriend to turn up by train to Godalming station. The train was late, we were bored and freezing and therefore, to entertain us both, I decided make us laugh to keep us warm.....I am still of the opinion that laughter keeps you warm....

VENETIA WALKEY

Small Holdings

This land is hand sewn - not machine made,
The rice hand stitched,
The flowers and little plants embroidered,
Planted tenderly with love and hope,
Appropriate Deities appealed to
And offerings made.
Nothing is left to chance.

Sudden Storm

The wind excites me,
It has not stirred all day,
Exhausted by the heat -
But now refreshed, leaps up,
Sensing the coming of the rain,
Scattering everything in its wake;
Doors banging, pots flying,
Chickens scurrying for shelter
Under the somnolent trees,
Their branches sighing, stirring ,
Wakening, as the wind flies across the fields
To embrace the rain.

RICHARD WILLIAMS

Back Stories

Tell me about the ones who wear red,
the *Star Trek* officers who only appear
in single episodes,
Tell me the lives that they once had
before they beamed down
to their stories' end.
What of the SWAT teams
in action movies,
taking a bullet so the hero can win,
or the secret ops troops
In prime time *Primeval*
who always end up being eaten
by something from the Cretaceous;
were they told that this could happen
when they went for the job interview,
did they get a final salary pension scheme
BUPA and life cover,
25 days holiday and a company car,
or did they moan the benefits were crap
and get the bus to work?
I want to know what they did on their days off,
did they go drinking with their mates
playing pool as if their youth would always last,
did they live in a pad in the city
surviving on microwave meals for one ,
was there a girl they were about to propose to,
did they dream of growing old together,
or was there a wife at home,
a mortgage in the suburbs
dinner in the oven,
burning as the news sank in,
a son asleep upstairs.

It Was Only His Second Ever Day Of Being Seven...

...and he was having a gob-stopper as a treat after a swimming lesson. They were waiting for his sisters to finish getting changed. His father was trying to read the paper. The economic outlook was not good. An election was near. Pompey were about to get relegated. Rolling the sweet around the roof of his mouth, he held it out between his teeth. "What colour is it, Dad? " he said. "Red, the colour of lava spewing out of the earth, or that Kit-Kat wrapper," his father replied, pointing towards the floor near a bin in the corner. The boy laughed. A few moments later, between the local and international news, he asked again, "What colour now?" His father looked up." Orange, the colour of the sun sliding over the horizon, or a bottle of Lucozade from the drinks machine" The boy smiled. Skipping the letters page, his father had a half-hearted go at the Sudoku. "What now?" "Yellow, the colour of sand on a tropical beach, or a packet of Starburst." The gob-stopper had shrunk considerably the next time he asked, somewhere in the editorial comments. "Green, a canopy of trees, just after rain, or a bottle of Sprite", came the answer. As the minutes slipped past, they kept going, through Football, Rugby and Motor Sport , each time the boy asking the same question, as the world in his mouth got smaller. "Blue, for the sea on a Bounty bar wrapper"; "Indigo, for a packet of pickled onion monster munch"; Violet, for the colour of dark, an hour before dawn. Asking again, his exasperated father replied "What colour do you want it to be? It can be any colour you want. You decide." The boy opened his mouth and held the small globe of sugar on the tip of his tongue. It was white, all colours and no colour, like a ball of light at the beginning of time. The boy tipped back his head, swallowed it whole.

Richard Williams

Page 23 of the Marathon Runner's Handbook – *Personal Safety*

It's the out of control ones
the head in the cloud ones
the head up their own arse ones
the out on the piss last night ones
the back from the club ones
the having a snog ones
(even at this time in the morning)
the it's not mine guv ones
the couldn't give a toss ones
the having a fag ones
the rolling a joint ones
the listening to rap ones
the listening to Rachmaninov ones
the gabbling on the mobile ones
the arguing with the kids ones
the swearing at the other half ones
the mad and the bad ones
the sane and the sad ones.

It's not the dogs you have to worry about,
it's the owners.

ISABEL WHITE

Things We Used To Do

North by the Railway, south the Motors,
Falla's Blue Bird,
or Watson's grey;
ubiquitous Albion
you took me,
via the teapot church,
to L'Ancresse and Vazon Bay.

76 trombones ringing in my ears,
thinking of Bobby's sailboat ride.
Fifty years on,
like the tide, ebbing away;
I think of those things we used to do
back in '62
when buses were always red or green or blue.

JANICE WINDLE

Alice In Officeland
(after “Jabberwocky” by Lewis Carroll)

‘Twas Friday and the compulads
Did clickle on the scribblescreens.
All dunwit were the bossybulls
in shirtyes red and green.

The ofterbore had uttered jokes
Until the air was buggerblue.
The secreladies gogglegigged
At lunch till half-past two.

Is it five-thirty? or dirty-dive?
And is the weekly shammock o’er?
Will compulads and secreladies
Go frickle at the watering-bore?

She thigh-toed out the greeded door
With primarked elegance and ease
Escorted by a bossybull
Who thought she was a fertish tease.

They fraggered down the crowdrubbed street
To Binny’s Vino Barisette,
He sat her in a claustrobooth
and fetched her gin and anisette.

“It’s growing late,” the secregirl
protested as he brought her more.
“Come bibblebibe, he urged her,
“Have a Screwdledrive, a Peridore.”

And so the night went woofing by,
“Let’s boddirub,” he said to her.
They found a room in Palmer’s Green,
And fiddle-fingered up the stairs.

"Come to my arms, my Bossyboy!
Tell me you have no wookywife!"
He told her bylines, spun a tale
about a singlifying life.

But suddenly the door bursts wide,
His wookywife stands bloring there
With lawdivorcers at her side …
"Alice, don't fall off that chair –

Where is that work I'm waiting for?
That database to be completed?
There's work to do, or there's the door!"

My fantasy ..... deleted

Queen Caroline's Bed

Today we visit Hampton Court.
here is Queen Caroline's bed.
She conceived three sons under
that silk-hung canopy.
Tonight I dream of her apartments
and of you. I remember
salt and porcelain in my silk-lined mouth.
I paint. Shining volume blossoms
at the tease of my brush.

Dear Robert Hass

Thank you for
the white egret
and for
the colours of
California where you
dream your life awake.
I slept
after you told
me about the boy with
the gun

*

Afterwards
I woke poised
between my love's hand
and my own
where they
interlaced
across the space
between our sleep-
numbed bodies
my foot hooked
under his
my head nested
next to his open
dreaming mouth

*

my breast under his
warm palm
his breath on
my calm fingers

*

I hope to see you again soon
when I have woken up some more

KAREN WITHECOMB

Pavilion Gardens

Piebald, dappled light and shade in verdant colours, silvered lime and nearly black,
Shifting with the zephyr ripples of the summer breezes, light and fair blown from the sea.
Dots and knots of people in their June-new clothes sprawled on the grass; a lazy pause.
The groups and families so timeless, like old days out of the long dead caught in a Frenchman's oils.
Impressionistic dashes of the paisley silk draped hippy pants, a ginger head, a striped beach ball.
This modern dejeuner sur l'herbe consisting of a plastic dish, no nudity and the great, great taste of diet Coke.
The sun burns just the same, the sun still gazes down implacably, its Aztec, blinding face expressionless.
A high-pitched tension marks the younger rings of eaters, drinkers, carves them right away from all the rest.
They have their textbooks, marker pens, their wan smiles and their chatter much too jittery.
And something in the cast-aside and well-thumbed nature of those books provides a clue to this strange fuss.
This lovely day of fresh green leaves and turquoise skies and salty breezes from the sea and lands afar
Is that one day that you remember with the friends whom travelled with you through this rite, soon to be lost.
This is the last exam day, last ever school day, final Final as the undergraduate pupating out of puberty at last.
The man in that old floppy hat with slo-mo hands enjoying his Tai Chi is smiling, he knows who he is.
As my thighs overheat within the faded sausage skins of my black jeans and that white disc stares hard.
And the boy with the dreadlocks and the woven top does juggling tricks, he's grown a beard to ape grown-up.
We sit in circles, lay like willing corpses strewn about a Royal garden from the past, as though our coup went wrong.

Still overseen by that preposterous confection, that pavilion too much
like a plopping castle made from dampened sand.
The teardrop falling domes, pot-bellied Regency themselves extruded
from a giant icing bag.
The music's free, the boy can play, boy, yeah the boy can play we say
and nod and close our eyes.
And crushed lawns smell of summer and the air is thick with skunk
and barbeques and sound.
We feel the freedom of our souls, luxuriate like potentates omnipotent
in our made up tents.
Scattering detritus like fat Buddhas whilst awkward gangs of foreign
language students envy us.
Standing, hot and bothered in uncertain groups with backpacks
uniform and cursing lack of British rain.
A seagull, bigger than a puppy , terrorises sandwich eaters, cocks his
head and gives us all the evil eye.
And I muse, stupefied by calories and starch and sunshine, on how it
is that all gulls' head are quite so white.
And, turning, wonder at fraternal toddler twins, unsteady and a
duplicate of hollowed backs and drunken, chubby gait.
Snippets of conversation overheard consumed like token rollups and
their drifting sense is so much smoke.
The older ladies with their pastel dresses and their pastel hair in post-
war curls sit by the cafeteria.
They occupy the deck chairs and the upright chairs with tables
wrought and brought the tea and cakes.
Polite applause accompanies another one of some large size as she
completes a song I failed to hear,
And as I struggle to my feet using my hand to push me up, I know the
days of sitting on the grass are few.
I look towards the ladies with their friends, all grey and only yesterday
in pigtails, giggling, married, mothers, now.
The days of tea and cakes are drawing near, of rattling teapot lids and
creaking bones and scones.
But I'll sit on the ground whilst I am able, listen to guitar and drama
of the last sweet days and lost dear friends.

GREG FREEMAN

Atalanta Ballroom

Between the Red House pub and the Railway Hotel,
after Ready, Steady, Go!, the rendezvous.
Handbags circled like wagons, tactical
retreats to the loos. Revving up scooters,
putting on that brave face, puffing on fags,
waiting for ever to make your first move.

Perfume, sweat, sprung floor sticky with beer;
Motown beat of my heart. Forces' sweethearts
starting fights, spilt drinks, innocent squaddies
tumbling bewildered into bloodied streets,
while not-yet-famous bands played on.
Most saw their names in lights.

Why didn't we? Things you'd forgotten with the years;
tunes in the head, words that once made sense.
Where can she be? Fingers tapping keys.
Hands searching in the dark, November bright with stars.
The longest kiss you've ever known;
holding each other on the last bus home

Surbiton Lagoon

for Graham Wood

Bewitching, between-the-wars poster
celebrating dazzling, endless summers.
Picture it: bikinis, towels, diving board,
slide, illicit fags on concrete terraces,
seventies heatwave buses disgorging
shouting, truanting queues day after day.
Anyone would think we had a right to it.
The sun, I mean; and maybe, to play.

The water was so cold it made you gasp.
Then in 1980 clouds came over,
the weather changed, the lido closed.
The pool, in an eerie after-life
filled with murky green water,
security-guarded by shivering bushes.
Asbestos lurked in abandoned buildings.
A forbidden, forgotten planet.

Bulldozers moved in; now it's
an estate of houses. Just a trace
of our lost lido, bewildering to the young:
bus stop still says "Surbiton Lagoon."
But if you've an ear, just listen:
on a sweltering summer's day
you can still hear shrieks
of laughter, many streets away.

JAMES WOOD

Poem

I sat in the bath
with her
and her ex-lovers
talking about
jokes
sounds
that I thought were ours

she told me a story
I can't remember
a fuck was on the cards
and I thought that
loves
are a bricolage
of all that's come before
maybe better

maybe worse

she said that, as a child,
she was starved of affection
I smiled
said nothing
and turned her into a glutton

Kōan

'Look at me' she gasped
as she came
as if to say
yes
I have fucked others
and will fuck more
but this, now,
tonight,
this is all I want.

GLOSSOPHOBIA

Um…

James Wood

About the Contributors

(alphabetical order)

Ingrid Andrew is a cat lover, artist, poet, and sometime singer songwriter. For many years she has designed the monthly posters for Survivors poetry, (an organization which celebrates the creative expression of the survivors of mental and emotional distress) and has often performed at the monthly Poetry Cafe gathering in London. ingridandrew.wordpress.com

Richard Alleyne is a former athlete from Barbados who came to the UK 23 years ago to study athletics with the British Amateur Athletic Association. He has been living in Woking, Surrey, for the last ten years. He started to play around with words from the age of ten.

The Antipoet, Paul Eccentric and Ian Newman, are together the world's finest exponents of beatrantin' rhythm 'n views! Having become enormously successful over the past five years, they now run their own nights in both London and the home counties. They have tirelessly toured the poetry, comedy and music circuits, and have appeared at countless festivals. They have also performed at magazine launches, Christmas light switch-ons, street parties, several libraries and schools, a shop window, the back of a lorry, on various boats, in the minstrel gallery of the Liverpool Town Hall and at Silverstone for the Grand Prix.

David Ashford is a poet in Somerstown. For the past six years he has run poetry events for the University of Surrey. He is general editor of Contraband Books. His most recent poem, *XARAGMATA*, was published last year by Veer Books.

Bryan Baker is quite tall and wears glasses. He used to live just off the Walworth Road in south London but he doesn't now. He paints. His poems have appeared in Fin, South Bank Poetry and The Delinquent.

Sally J Blackmore has been writing poetry seriously for twelve years and has published two anthologies, '*Random*' and '*Deployed*', both available from Behindthehighstreet.co.uk. Sally blogs regularly at www.sallyjblackmore.co.uk and holds poetry workshops in her Surrey writing room.

Claire Booker was born in Guildford, Surrey. Her stage plays have been produced in Australia, Europe, America and the UK and she has had radio plays broadcast on Radio 4 and LBC. She is a member of Clapham-based 'Original Poets' and has guested at a number of spoken word events. Her poems have appeared in Magma, the Morning Star, New Welsh Review, Prole and Rialto among others. More info at www.bookerplays.co.uk

Stephen Boyce has been published widely in magazines and online and has won a number of awards. He is the author of two collections, *Desire Lines* (Arrowhead 2010) and *The Sisyphus Dog* (Worple 2014), "… a master of the simple but telling phrase." He is a trustee of Winchester Poetry Festival.
www.stephenboycepoetry.co.uk.

Graham Brown was born in Aldershot in 1953. Has written poetry since 1976 and has appeared at many venues including the Hastings National Poetry Festival. Ran 'Stand and Deliver' Open Mic in Newcastle between 1996 and 2000. Now lives on the Isle of Wight and performs at events in Southampton, Portsmouth, Reading and Guildford and anywhere else that will have him!

Graham Buchan has published poetry (*Airport Reading, There is Violence in these Vapours, In Bed with Shostakovich,* all from The Tall Lighthouse), short stories, travel writing and many film and art reviews. He has read in London, southern England, New York, Austin and Vancouver. Professionally he writes and directs factual films.

Ernie Burns

Ernie Burns is a London based poet, songwriter, playwright and performer. Performing regularly since the early naughties., he has run and hosted several poetry nights in London and currently co-comperes Platform 1 every second Saturday at the Poetry Cafe in Covent Garden. He utilizes many styles, aiming to entertain using quirky wit and left-field insight.

Nancy Charley lives in Ramsgate. Her poetry collection *This Woman* was published by Conversation Paperpress in 2012. She has performed her poetry at theatres, arts centres and pubs, for Human Rights, New Writing Nights and for the sheer enjoyment. In 2013 she toured her one-woman show, *Patricia's Box*.

David Cooke won a Gregory Award in 1977 and published his first collection, *Brueghel's Dancers* in 1984. His collection, *In the Distance*, was published in 2011 by Night Publishing and a collection of more recent pieces, *Work Horses*, was published by Ward Wood Publishing in 2012. His poems and reviews have appeared widely in journals.

Dónall Dempsey was born in the Curragh in Ireland and was Ireland's first Poet in Residence in a secondary school. He has appeared on Irish television and radio and has read and performed all over England and in Scotland. He now lives in Guildford and hosts 'Pop Up Poetry' Spoken Word at the Bar des Arts. Dónall's poems have been published in numerous journals and anthologies and he has published three collections of poems, the most recent being "The Smell of Purple" (2014).

Alex de Suys "The Real Thang" host, Baron von Susius "Vee leave ze cuvverz to uvverz!" is better known as Alex de Suys and can occasionally be seen lowering the tone in certain Guildford wine bars where London performers of his acquaintance introduce regular new crowds to poetry and that. "I just pop in for the abuse" quips Al. "Donall, Give me back my feckin' jacket."

Louise Etheridge is a professional copywriter who specialises in funny and quirk but can do normal, too. She spends her time conserving her energy and playing with her friends. She likes to write ridiculous verse just because. She has two books out on Amazon - *Slightly Wrong*, her first collection of disturbing and funny verse, and *Happy Stories for Busy People*, which are happy stories for busy people. She also writes comedy lyrics to songs you know, and leads the popular rude acapella girl group, The Dirty Carols. More information about Louise at www.louiseetheridge.com, www.facebook/LouiseDoesWords and www.facebook/TheDirtyCarols.

Marian Fielding used to be a probation officer (Simon Armitage was too!) She has also acted with the Tower Theatre and performed a one woman play for Unity Theatre's comeback, (but then they disappeared again...) She has failed to finish two novels but has had several short stories published. Her poetry has been published in *The Interpreter's House, South, South Bank Poetry, Orbis* and the *Pop Up Anthology 2013.*

Peter Fisher was born in Fareham, Hampshire. He writes poems, flash fiction, short stories and novels. He likes to perform some of his work as the opportunities arise. He says, "I like being a writer; it's something I can do while sitting on my backside."

Neil Flatman has had poems published in written and audio form and in a number of journals online, including The Poetry Storehouse.

Cathy Flower, performance poet [Poet for Life] began her quest to write and deliver her poetry in Sydney, 1991. She has performed in numerous venues across Australia. Cathy arrived in East London in 2004, continuing her poetry vocation. She continues to write and extensively performs in London on radio and a plethora of performance spaces. More information can be found at www.cathypoetflower.tumblr.com

Greg Freeman has had poems published in several magazines and anthologies, and in the Morning Star. He is a former newspaper sub-editor, and now news editor for the poetry website Write Out Loud.

Andy V Frost is a 52-year-old Merton-based Biker who has been writing and performing poetry for the past thirteen years. His favourite things after motorcycles and any excuse to ride them are; all good music, good cinema, live poetry, natural beauty and kites. He has often been found at the side of the road writing to the rhythm of his engine with a fly-peppered smile on his face.

Robert Garnham is a performance poet. Originally from Surrey, he now lives in Devon. He performs regularly in Devon and London and is the reigning Exeter Poetry Slam Champion. He has supported John Hegley in London and worked with some of the top names in performance poetry.

Mark Gilfillan (**aka the Stokey Bard**) was born in Sheffield, South Yorkshire. He moved down to London in 1987. He performs his work in many venues in the city and is the author of '*Ballistic Kisses*', a collection of poems, clerihews, poems for tots and artworks. He is the founder and host of *Big Mouth*, a regular performance evening at the Mascara Bar in Stoke Newington.

Graham Goddard (Oh Standfast) lives in London. When not volunteering/running/writing for CALM, a fantastic charity that tackles the complicated subject of male suicide Graham can often be found onstage performing poetry under the guise of 'rant rhyming agitated wordsmith' All profit from sales of his book, *Don't you wish your Kindle was a book like me?* will be donated to CALM. (Available at £3 by visiting http://ohstandfast.wordpress.com/shop)

Grim Chip - Grim Chip has been knocking about London poetry stages, as 'The Bro's Grim', for a while. Once seen, never forgotten, his compelling live work belies the craft in his writing. Whether tackling the personal or the political his poems bristle and snap, never failing to hit the mark.

Sue Guiney is an American writer based in London. Her publications include 2 poetry collections and 3 novels. She is now writing a series of novels set in present day Cambodia where she founded and teaches a writing workshop for at-risk children called "Writing Through Cambodia".

Roya Hamid is a dramatherapist, "A dramatherapist, clinical supervisor, storyteller, project designer, group facilitator and founder of Marvellous Productions a creative arts organisation specialising in play, engagement and communication skills oh yeah and a mother of two daughters. Her website is www.marvellousproductions.com

Gary W Hartley performs under the name of **Gary from Leeds.** Originally trained as a journalist, he is co-editor of *The Alarmist*, a literary journal. In summer 2014 he performed his show *"Yeti"* at the Edinburgh Festival Fringe.

A F Harrold is an English poet, children's author and performer. More information can be found at www.afharrold.com.

Janis Haves – Tea-aholic, workaholic, high strung, laid back, often over the top, regularly under the wire, head in the clouds, back against the wall poet, singer/songwriter and relentless optimist.

Fran Isherwood can often be found flinging herself around the Spoken Word scene's stages and hosts a monthly poetry event in East London. Her poetry is a wry, awry, word-playful gallop through the vagaries of life encountering mail-stealing snails, lollipop ladies, Glam

Rock, insomnia and macabre part-time jobs en route. She hosts a regular poetry night, *"Girlfriend in a Comma'* at the Full Stop Bar in London.

Ghareeb Iskander is an Iraqi poet based in London. He has published seven books including *A Chariot of Illusion* (Exiled Writers Ink, 2009); *Gilgamesh's Snake*(Beirut, 2012) which is now being translated into English; *Translating Sayyab into English* (London, 2013). He has taken part in Erbil, Reel Iraq, Edinburgh, Wigtown, Bath and Niniti festivals.

Karen Izod is an Organisational Consultant, Academic and Writer, living in Guildford. She is a lover of birds and wild-places.

Martin Jones is married and has two children, now grown up. He has spent many years as a teacher, first in comprehensive schools in London, then in teacher training college in Nigeria, then in a further education college in Weybridge, Surrey. He is a long-standing member of the Wey Poets, Guildford, and a joint editor of the magazine. His poems have appeared in numerous magazines.

Mel Jones is a winner of the PBS Free Fringe Best Spoken Word Show award, a multiple slam and superslam champion and a regular feature performer on the London poetry scene. She is co-host of the Friggers of Speech event in Crouch End and author of the very naughty poetry collection, 'Mmmmm'

Anna Kahn runs around London reciting poetry and having fun. She can often be found in the company of people who should know better.

Wendy Klein, a retired psychotherapist, was born in the US too long ago to remember. She has been writing poetry since 2000, has won many prizes and is widely published in magazines and anthologies, with two full collections from Cinnamon Press: 'Cuba in the Blood' (2009) and 'Anything in Turquoise,' (2013).

Sue Kucko says, 'Pop up Poetry finally gave me a chance to perform in public, so after all these years (and in homage to Doris Day and of course my best friend Debs) I was able to sing my version of the Calamity Jane classic.....' Sue has worked at the Bar des Arts and supported Pop Up since 2012.

Andy B J Low says:
"Who am I? No one knows. Professional idiot I suppose.
Romantic tart, tender heart. I love beautiful things.
That'll do for a start.
But be careful what else you ask of me.
The clue's in the e-mail: Dr.Evil.Phd(@outlook.com)"

Holly Luhning is a novelist and poet. She is the author of a collection of poetry (Sway, Thistledown Press, 2004) and two chapbooks (Plush, Jack Pine Press, 2006 and Pharmacoi; or A Mechanical Account of Poisons in Several Essays, Contraband, 2013) as well as a novel (Quiver, HarperCollins, 2011). Her work has appeared in various anthologies and journals, and she also writes critically on eighteenth-century print culture and theories of the body. She is a lecturer in Creative Writing at the University of Surrey and lives in London.

Tracey Marion is a genderqueer, bisexual zinester who writes about politics, everyday life and surviving with mental illness. They enjoy awkward rhymes, marmite and making things out of yarn. Tracey has been spoken wording since 2007 and written wording since they could do their ABCs.

Alwyn Marriage has been a university lecturer, chief executive of two NGOs, Editor of a journal and an Environmental Consultant. Three of her seven published books have been poetry, and her work appears frequently in magazines and anthologies. She is now Managing Editor of Oversteps Books, holds a research fellowship at the University of Surrey, was Poet in Residence for the Winchester 10 Days Arts Festival 2013 and gives readings all over Britain and abroad. www.marriages.me.uk/alwyn.htm

Amy McAllister is an award-winning poet from Dublin. She has been poet-in-residence for *Transport for London* and at *Bang Said the Gun*, was selected to read from the restored manuscript of Sylvia Plath's *Ariel* at the *Royal Festival Hall* alongside Plath's daughter Frieda Hughes, and her poetry is published in *Rhyming Thunder*, *South Bank Poetry Magazine*, and *Outwest*. Her own collection is coming out at the end of 2014. amymcallisterpoetry.wordpress.com

Jennifer A McGowan, when she is not hiding in the fifteenth century, publishes poetry and prose in many magazines and anthologies on both sides of the Atlantic, including *Agenda* and *Acumen.* Her chapbooks are available from Finishing Line Press. Her website can be found at http://www.jenniferamcgowan.com .

Patrick Osada is an editor, reviewer of poetry and a member of the Management Team for South Poetry Magazine. His current collection, *Choosing The Route* , is published in England by Indigo Dreams Publishing.
For more information : www.poetry-patrickosada.co.uk

Mary Pargeter has recently published her first collection, *'Journey in Shades'*, re-visiting her childhood, loss of innocence, love, heartbreak and death, and reflects with admirable frankness on those universal rites of passage common to us all. Reviews of her book include: "I have felt engaged with the work, and responsive to its emotional charge." *Professor Carol Rumens Guardian Books Online*; "She lets detail speak, often exquisitely, through things as they are; there is no attempt to escape through fantasy." *Jay Ramsay, Poetry Editor, Caduceus*

Ed Parshotam - Coming to spoken word via hip-hop music, Ed Parshotam delivers mind-bending intricate rhymes that take the listener on a whirlwind journey, from the funny and light-hearted to the poignant and reflective - and back again.

Geoffrey Pimlott, a painter who exhibits regularly around the UK, started writing poetry six years ago, encouraged by a writers' group in Chiang Mai, Thailand, Writers Without Borders. He reads his poems at Pop Up Poets, Bar Des Arts, Guildford, where he also has an exhibition of his watercolours in their first floor gallery space.

Lorri Pimlott lives in Reigate. She was partly brought up in New Zealand and Australia, and has since lived in Papua New Guinea, Thailand and France. She often draws on her experiences of these widely-different cultures in her poetry. Other sources of inspiration include her interest in history and her love of plants.

Bethany W Pope is an award-winning author of the LBA, and a finalist for the Faulkner-Wisdom Awards. She was a runner up for the Cinnamon Press Novel Competition. She received her PhD from Aberystwyth University's Creative Writing program. Her first poetry collection, *A Radiance*, was published by Cultured Llama Press in June 2012. Her second collection, *Crown of Thorns*, was published by Oneiros press in 2013. The Gospel of Flies, was released in 2014 and her next collection, *Undisturbed Circles,* will be released by Lapwing Press this December.

Steve Pottinger has gigged the length and breadth of the country, in pubs and clubs, at poetry nights and festivals. His latest book is "*Island Songs*". He loves words, loves people more, and enjoys poetry which makes him smile, or think, or want to man the barricades. When not standing behind a microphone or in front of an audience, he can often be found down the pub. He hopes you enjoy his work. More information is at www.stevepottinger. co.uk.

Cat Randle Cat Randle has performed poetry all over the South East. She has created the Teapoets Collective along with Syd Meats and runs a poetry cafe in Romsey. Currently she is writing an adult novel about her steam punk creation Merciful Grace. You can find her on Facebook as Cat Randle.

Stephen Ross is an Award winning Irish poet who was born in 1972. Following graduation from Edinburgh University and his eventual disillusionment with corporate life he returned to Ireland to unwind, unwaged. In 2010 Stephen had an extraordinary experience whereupon he first began to receive and write poetry. He was awarded the Tir na Saor Poet Laureate in 2013.

Chrys Salt has published three full poetry collections and four pamphlets. Her work has appeared in many anthologies and has been performed on Radio 3 and 4, UK wide, in the USA, Canada, France, Germany and Finland. It has been translated into French and Arabic and is currently being translated into Hebrew. *The Burning* from *Weaver of Grass* was selected as one of the 20 Best Scottish Poems 2012. In 2014 her pamphlet *Weaver of Grass* was shortlisted for the Callum Macdonald Memorial Award, she was awarded a Writers Bursary by Creative Scotland to finish her next collection and awarded an MBE in the Queen's Birthday Honours List.

Pauline Sewards found her poetry voice in London and now lives in Bristol. She has been published in several small press magazines including *South Bank Poetry*, *Loose Muse* and *Ariadne's Threaa* and has read work at many venues including the Poetry Cafe in Covent Garden and the Torriano in Camden.

Shadwell Smith scribbles on Post-It notes, portions of anatomy and even on tropical fruit. He isn't afraid to use the odd cultural reference in his poetry. His poems have appeared in *Snakeskin, Ink, Sweat and Tears, London Grip, Prole, Poetry WTFyour bio reads*
and *Message in a Bottle.*

Elaine Stabler says: I am currently a student of the University of Surrey, studying English Literature with Creative Writing. Within this year alone I have already achieved so much, including; starting my own Creative Writing Society within my University, of which I am Chairman. And I have performed my poetry alongside the current UK slam poetry champion, Sara Hirsch. And I'm not done yet – watch this space!

Paul Sutherland is an award-winning poet/writer, British-Canadian by birth (UK resident since 1973) and has had
published eight collections, and poems in journals, anthologies, and on websites. Founding editor of *Dream Catcher* literary magazine. Writes fiction, leads creative writing workshops and retreats (for different abilities and ages). Frequently performs his poems. He has been freelance since 2004. 'He became a Sufi Muslim in 2004. Under the name of Paul Abdul Wadud Sutherland, his collection *Poems on the Life of the Prophet Muhammad (saws)* has just been published,
(Muslim Academic Trust. 2014)

Thomas Thurman entered the world in 1975, yet shows no sign of running out of things to discover. He may also be found fixing computers or writing story-books. His ambition is to find the secret of becoming a squirrel so that he can hide in trees and compose sonnets all winter.

Gareth Toms says, 'I met Jan and Dónall last November when they signed-up for the open-mic event which I hosted at Tongues and Grooves tenth anniversary celebrations in Portsmouth. They in turn, invited me to read at Pop-Up Poetry for twenty minutes, but due to some enthusiastic audience participation it stretched to twenty seven. My work was recently described as, "*. . . refreshingly down to earth and completely unpretentious.*" '

Kathy Tytler says, 'I am a long distance runner from Reading and I consider the scenery to be just as important as the race. From my view at the back I have plenty of time to find inspiration to write *Running Poetry.* I aim to bring Poetry to Runners and Runners to Poetry... and maybe even Poets to Running!!

Thomas Vliestra started writing in 2009 while studying Psychology at the University of Surrey. He began performing Spoken Word and Poetry, alongside working with his peers to create Acoustic Hip Hop under the name Tom V & Friends. Since graduating he has been using his interest in poetry in therapeutic work in the practice where he is a case worker. He continues to write and returns to read at Pop Up whenever he can.

Venetia Walkey studied sculpture at Guildford College of Art. She now lives in Thailand. Her unorthodox sculptures lead us on a journey from Ignorance to Enlightenment via the Buddhist Pathway to Peace at Dhamma Park, which she created in North Thailand. Her poems have popped up at the Bar des Arts.

Isabel White performs all over the UK, hails from the North, lives in the South (traitor!) and loves the opportunity to spread her anarchic mash ups to new audiences, including the wonderful Bar Des Arts. Widely published and recent runner up in the BBC Radio 3 Proms competition, she also curates poetry events in partnership with Platform-7.

Janice Windle lives, writes and paints her canvases in Guildford, UK. She has had poems and short fiction published online and in print anthologies and literary magazines. She won third prize in the Segora Poetry competition 2013. She has published three collection of her poems, one of which she illustrated with her own watercolour paintings.

Karen Withecomb hosts *Shine So Hard*, a weekly open mic night in Brighton, where she lives and works. Karen is a prolific poet and a frequent performer of her work.

James Wood is a student at the University of York; he writes words down in a funny order and calls them poems. He likes jazz, eggs and pennies. He hates poems, shoes and bacon. He is a word game.

The Contributors
(coloured photographs on the cover)

	Claire Booker	Gareth Toms	Alwyn Marriage	Ghareeb Iskander	Pete Fisher	Shadwell Smith
Ed Parshotam	Anna Kahn	Cat Randle	Richard Williams	Elaine Stabler	Greg Freeman	Graham Buchan
Andy V Frost	Steve Pottinger	Holly Luhning	Marian Fielding	Bethany Pope	Thomas Thurman	Kathy Tytler
Ernie Burns		Thomas Vliestra	Chrys Salt	David Ashford	Patrick Osada	Cathy Flower
(The Antipoet) Paul Eccentric	Neil Flatman	A F Harrold	Dónall Dempsey	Richard Alleyne	Wendy Klein	Robert Garnham
Sally Blackmore	Paul Sutherland	Ingrid Andrew	Janis Haves	Grim Chip		Mark Gilfillan (The Stokey Bard)
Karen Izod	Andy B J Low	Lorri Pimlott	Graham Brown	Martin Jones	Sue Guiney	Louise Etheridge
Sue Kucko	Fran Isherwood	Stephen Ross	Alex De Suys	Gary W Hartley (Gary from Leeds)	Mel Jones	Graham Goddard (Oh Standfast)
Tracey Marion	Jennifer McGowan	Geoffrey Pimlott	Janice Windle	Karen Withecomb	Bryan Baker	Pauline Sewards
David Cooke	Roya Hamid	Amy McAllister	Isabel White	Stephen Boyce	Mary Pargeter	

ACKNOWLEDGEMENTS

Shooting The Greys by Alwyn Marriage was first published in *Broadsheet*, 2013.
Overload by Alwyn Marriage was first published in *Domestic Cherry*, 2013.
Lycra by Alwyn Marriage was first published in *Spokes*, Otley Word Feast Anthology.

It Was Only His Second Ever Day Of Being Seven... by David Williams was previously published in *Portsmouth Writers to Watch* and *Orbis Poetry Magazine.*
Back Stories by David Williams was previously published in *Writers to Watch, Portsmouth*, and *Ariadne's Thread.*

Knokke Le *Zoute* by Stephen Boyce is from his collection *Desire Lines* (Arrowhead 2010).
Escapement by Stephen Boyce was first published in *Magma 57.*
Vital Signs and ***Counting The Pips*** by Stephen Boyce are from his collection *Sisyphus Dog* (Worple, 2014).

Soldier by Sally Blackmore was shortlisted for the Fish Poetry Prize.

Not Me by Marion Fielding was first published in *South Magazine.*
The Pea by Marion Fielding was first published in *The Interpreter's House*

On the Red Light by Patrick Osada is from his collection *Close to the Edge.*
Wild Ransoms by Patrick Osada is from his collection *Rough Music.*
Presence by Patrick Osada is the final poem in his current collection, *Choosing the Route.*

Classification: Ursus consolativus by Nancy Charley won the Saveas poetry competition 2014.

My Water Bottle by Sue Guiney was published in *South Issue 48.*
Mekong Women by Sue Guiney was published in *In Protest: 150 Poems for Human Rights.*

Himself by Wendy Klein was published on Hilda Sheehan's blog, *'Amaryllis'.*
Red Toenails in April was highly commended and ***The Million Women Minus One*** by Wendy Klein was commended in the Torriano Competition.

Things We Used To Do by Isabel White was selected for inclusion in their programme *Poems on the Buses 2014* by Guernsey International Literary Festival.

Other Dempsey & Windle publications:

Anti-Gravity by Janice Windle (2011)

How to Make a Dress out of Silence by Janice Windle (2012)

Sifting Sound into Shape by Dónall Dempsey (2012)

Sticky Ends and Squiggles by Janice Windle (2013)

Loving the Light by Janice Windle (2013)

The Pop Up Anthology 2013 edited by Janice Windle

Being Dragged Across the Carpet by the Cat by Dónall Dempsey (2013)

dempseyandwindle.co.uk

www.ingramcontent.com/pod-product-compliance
Ingram Content Group UK Ltd.
Pitfield, Milton Keynes, MK11 3LW, UK
UKHW040602210726
13854UKWH00008B/1807

9 781907 435249